The Respiratory System

YOUR BODY How It Works

Cells, Tissues, and Skin

The Circulatory System

Human Development

The Immune System

The Reproductive System

The Respiratory System

The Respiratory System

Susan Whittemore, Ph.D.
Professor of Biology
Keene State College, Keene, N.H.

Introduction by
Denton A. Cooley, M.D.
President and Surgeon-in-Chief
of the Texas Heart Institute
Clinical Professor of Surgery at the
University of Texas Medical School, Houston, Texas

CHELSEA HOUSE
PUBLISHERS
A Haights Cross Communications Company
Philadelphia

CHELSEA HOUSE PUBLISHERS
VP, NEW PRODUCT DEVELOPMENT Sally Cheney
DIRECTOR OF PRODUCTION Kim Shinners
CREATIVE MANAGER Takeshi Takahashi
MANUFACTURING MANAGER Diann Grasse

Staff for THE RESPIRATORY SYSTEM
EDITOR Beth Reger
PRODUCTION EDITOR Megan Emery
PHOTO EDITOR Sarah Bloom
SERIES & COVER DESIGNER Terry Mallon
LAYOUT 21st Century Publishing and Communications, Inc.

www.chelseahouse.com

First Printing

1 3 5 7 9 8 6 4 2

Library of Congress Cataloging-in-Publication Data

Whittemore, Susan.
    The respiratory system / Susan Whittemore.
        v. cm. — (Your body, how it works)
    Includes index.
    Contents: Breathing thin air — The air we breathe: understanding our
atmosphere —Why do we breathe? — Anatomy of the respiratory system — The diffusion of gas molecules — How do we breathe? — Preventing collapse of the lungs — How the respiratory system adjusts to
meet changing oxygen demands — Respiratory disease.
    ISBN 0-7910-7627-X
    1. Respiratory organs—Juvenile literature. 2. Respiration—Juvenile
literature. [1. Respiratory system. 2. Respiration.] I. Title. II. Series.
    QP121.W45 2004
    612.2—dc22

                        2003025583

Table of Contents

Introduction

The human body is an incredibly complex and amazing structure. At best, it is a source of strength, beauty, and wonder. We can compare the healthy body to a well-designed machine whose parts work smoothly together. We can also compare it to a symphony orchestra in which each instrument has a different part to play. When all of the musicians play together, they produce beautiful music.

From a purely physical standpoint, our bodies are made mainly of water. We are also made of many minerals, including calcium, phosphorous, potassium, sulfur, sodium, chlorine, magnesium, and iron. In order of size, the elements of the body are organized into cells, tissues, and organs. Related organs are combined into systems, including the musculoskeletal, cardio-vascular, nervous, respiratory, gastrointestinal, endocrine, and reproductive systems.

Our cells and tissues are constantly wearing out and being replaced without our even knowing it. In fact, much of the time, we take our body for granted. When it is work-ing properly, we tend to ignore it. Although the heart beats about 100,000 times per day and we breathe more than 10 million times per year, we do not normally think about these things. When something goes wrong, however, our bodies tell us through pain and other symptoms. In fact, pain is a very effective alarm system that lets us know the body needs attention. If the pain does not go away, we may need to see a doctor. Even without medical help, the body has an amazing ability to heal itself. If we cut ourselves, the blood clotting system works to seal the cut right away, and the immune defense system sends out special blood cells that are programmed to heal the area.

During the past 50 years, doctors have gained the ability to repair or replace almost every part of the body. In my own field of cardiovascular surgery, we are able to open the heart and repair its valves, arteries, chambers, and connections. In many cases, these repairs can be done through a tiny "keyhole" incision that speeds up patient recovery and leaves hardly any scar. If the entire heart is diseased, we can replace it altogether, either with a donor heart or with a mechanical device. In the future, the use of mechanical hearts will probably be common in patients who would otherwise die of heart disease.

Until the mid-twentieth century, infections and contagious diseases related to viruses and bacteria were the most common causes of death. Even a simple scratch could become infected and lead to death from "blood poisoning." After penicillin and other antibiotics became available in the 1930s and '40s, doctors were able to treat blood poisoning, tuberculosis, pneumonia, and many other bacterial diseases. Also, the introduction of modern vaccines allowed us to prevent childhood illnesses, smallpox, polio, flu, and other contagions that used to kill or cripple thousands.

Today, plagues such as the "Spanish flu" epidemic of 1918–19, which killed 20 to 40 million people worldwide, are unknown except in history books. Now that these diseases can be avoided, people are living long enough to have long-term (chronic) conditions such as cancer, heart failure, diabetes, and arthritis. Because chronic diseases tend to involve many organ systems or even the whole body, they cannot always be cured with surgery. These days, researchers are doing a lot of work at the cellular level, trying to find the underlying causes of chronic illnesses. Scientists recently finished mapping the human genome, which is a set of coded "instructions" programmed into our cells. Each cell contains 3 billion "letters" of this code. By showing how the body is made, the human genome will help researchers prevent and treat disease at its source, within the cells themselves.

The body's long-term health depends on many factors, called risk factors. Some risk factors, including our age, sex, and family history of certain diseases, are beyond our control. Other important risk factors include our lifestyle, behavior, and environment. Our modern lifestyle offers many advantages but is not always good for our bodies. In western Europe and the United States, we tend to be stressed, overweight, and out of shape. Many of us have unhealthy habits such as smoking cigarettes, abusing alcohol, or using drugs. Our air, water, and food often contain hazardous chemicals and industrial waste products. Fortunately, we can do something about most of these risk factors. At any age, the most important things we can do for our bodies are to eat right, exercise regularly, get enough sleep, and refuse to smoke, overuse alcohol, or use addictive drugs. We can also help clean up our environment. These simple steps will lower our chances of getting cancer, heart disease, or other serious disorders.

These days, thanks to the Internet and other forms of media coverage, people are more aware of health-related matters. The average person knows more about the human body than ever before. Patients want to understand their medical conditions and treatment options. They want to play a more active role, along with their doctors, in making medical decisions and in taking care of their own health.

I encourage you to learn as much as you can about your body and to treat your body well. These things may not seem too important to you now, while you are young, but the habits and behaviors that you practice today will affect your physical well-being for the rest of your life. The present book series, YOUR BODY: HOW IT WORKS, is an excellent introduction to human biology and anatomy. I hope that it will awaken within you a lifelong interest in these subjects.

Denton A. Cooley, M.D.
President and Surgeon-in-Chief
of the Texas Heart Institute
Clinical Professor of Surgery at the
University of Texas Medical School, Houston, Texas

1

Breathing Thin Air

In May 1996, Jon Krakauer (Figure 1.1) was one of eight members of a guided expedition up Mount Everest, the world's tallest mountain. Although Krakauer eventually reached the summit, twelve other climbers who were on Everest during the same time period died, including four from his own expedition. Krakauer recounted this harrowing disaster in his book *Into Thin Air*.

Krakauer nearly died on Everest. As he was descending from the summit, he became concerned that his oxygen supply would run out before he could reach the uppermost camp where additional oxygen tanks were stored. He asked a fellow climber to turn off the oxygen valve on his back so he could conserve his remaining oxygen. Unfortunately, the climber inadvertently opened Krakauer's valve completely, and within minutes, his tank was completely out of oxygen. Krakauer described how he began to lose his eyesight and mental faculties immediately. He was fully aware that, in the absence of oxygen, his brain cells were dying at a rapid pace. He struggled to reach the encampment before he completely lost consciousness. It is evident from his ability to write this gripping tale that he suffered no substantial brain damage from his experience. Other climbers in Krakauer's situation have not been as lucky (Figure 1.2).

What is "thin air," and why is it so physiologically challenging for humans? Krakauer states in his book that all health risks associated with high-altitude environments are either due to or worsened by the low oxygen levels at those heights. Some climbers have returned from expeditions with permanent brain damage. Others have lost appendages and suffered extensive tissue damage due to hypothermia,

Figure 1.1 Jon Krakauer speaks with reporters about his ordeal on Mount Everest. He nearly died after running out of oxygen on his descent from the summit but was able to reach his camp just in time.

a potentially lethal condition in which the body temperature is lower than normal. Hypothermia occurs more rapidly in low-oxygen environments.

High-altitude pulmonary edema, or HAPE, is another dangerous ailment experienced by some high-altitude climbers. With HAPE, severe high blood pressure develops in the capillaries of the lungs, forcing fluid to leak into the air spaces

Figure 1.2 Climbing Mount Everest, as this man is doing, is very difficult due to the lack of oxygen as the climber gets higher. Expeditions to the summit must carry adequate supplies of oxygen to aid their members' survival.

of the lungs. The HAPE sufferer literally begins to drown in his or her own body fluids and may die if not treated immediately.

CONNECTIONS

In this book, you will learn about the physiological challenges associated with high altitude and other extreme environments. You will explore how the human body attempts to adapt to certain environmental challenges and learn why it is not always successful in these attempts. In the last chapter of this book, you will explore the physiological adaptations of humans, like the Sherpas, Tibetans, and Andeans, who have lived for generations at high altitude.

Human physiologists, scientists who study how the human body works, learn a great deal by studying the body both in health and with disease. Respiratory physiologists, those who specifically investigate the respiratory system and how it functions, are no exception. It is their significant, cumulative accomplishments that have provided the current wealth of information on the workings of this marvelous organ system.

2

The Air We Breathe: Understanding Our Atmosphere

EARTH'S ATMOSPHERE

To understand respiration, it is necessary to understand what is in air. Atmospheric air consists of a mixture of gases and other airborne molecules. The predominant gases are nitrogen (78%), oxygen (21%), and the **noble**, or inert, **gases** such as argon, neon, and helium (1%). These gases are also considered to be the permanent gases. Small amounts of variable gases, including water vapor, carbon dioxide, methane, and ozone, are also present.

The composition of Earth's atmosphere has changed significantly over the course of history. When Earth was initially formed, it was likely too hot to retain any atmosphere. Scientists believe that Earth's first atmosphere consisted of helium, hydrogen, ammonia, and methane. Water vapor, carbon dioxide, and nitrogen are thought to be the main constituents of Earth's second atmosphere, a result of the intense volcanic activity associated with that period of Earth's history.

The volcanoes released huge amounts of water vapor into Earth's atmosphere, resulting in cloud formation and rain. With time, water collected into reservoirs, including oceans, lakes, and rivers. Scientists believe that the carbon dioxide in the atmosphere was washed from the sky into these water reservoirs, where it became tied up chemically in the sediments. Because nitrogen is relatively chemically inert as compared to carbon dioxide, it remained in the atmosphere. As a result, nitrogen began to accumulate and eventually predominate in the atmosphere.

It is also believed that the intense solar radiation of that period was sufficient to split water vapor into hydrogen and oxygen. Like nitrogen, oxygen also began to accumulate in the atmosphere, while hydrogen gas, which is lighter, escaped Earth's atmosphere. The process of photosynthesis has also contributed to the oxygen levels of our atmosphere. These shifts in the gaseous composition of Earth's atmosphere occurred over billions of years. Human activity is now changing the composition of our atmosphere over much shorter time frames.

PARTIAL PRESSURES OF GASES

In a high-altitude environment like Mount Everest, the relative proportions of nitrogen, oxygen, and the other gases do not differ from their proportions at sea level (Figure 2.1). Oxygen represents almost 21% of the atmospheric gas molecules on the top of Mount Everest, just as it does at sea level. On the other hand, it is commonly known that it is more difficult to breathe on top of Mount Everest and that most climbers require the use of oxygen tanks to complete their climb. This example illustrates the fact that knowing the percentage of a gas in the atmosphere is not a useful measure of the actual amount of gas available for respiration.

Molecules of gas, such as oxygen (O_2) and nitrogen (N_2), are under continuous random motion and, as a result, exert a pressure. The pressure of a gas depends on two primary factors: temperature and the concentration of the gas (or the number of gas molecules per unit volume). **Dalton's Law** states that in a mixture of gases, such as atmospheric gas, the pressure exerted by each gas in the mixture is independent of the pressure exerted by the other gases. For this reason, the total pressure of a mixture of gases is equal to the sum of all the individual pressures, also known as the **partial pressures.**

THE COMPOSITION OF DRY AIR NEAR GROUND LEVEL	
GAS	AVERAGE PERCENTAGE BY VOLUME
NITROGEN	78.08
OXYGEN	20.95
ARGON	0.93
CARBON DIOXIDE	0.03
NEON	0.0018
HELIUM	0.00052
METHANE	0.00015
KRYPTON	0.00011
HYDROGEN, CARBON MONOXIDE, XENON, OZONE	<0.0001

Figure 2.1 The composition of dry atmospheric air is shown here. Although we call the air we breathe "oxygen," that element is actually the second most prevalent composite of air. Nitrogen is the most abundant gas in the air we breathe.

The partial pressure of a gas is directly proportional to the concentration of the gas (the number of gas molecules per unit volume). The symbol for partial pressure is a "P" in front of the structural formula for the gas. For example, PN_2 is a symbol for the partial pressure of nitrogen (N_2), and PO_2 represents the partial pressure of oxygen (O_2). The units for pressure typically used by human physiologists are "mm Hg," or millimeters of mercury. This unit of measure refers to the use of mercury-containing manometers to measure pressure.

REPORT CARD: U.S. PROGRESS ON IMPROVING AIR QUALITY

The average American breathes 3,400 gallons of air per day. In addition to gas molecules, such as oxygen and nitrogen, there are numerous other constituents of air. Some of these constituents can profoundly affect people's health. Air can contain infectious or disease-causing agents, such as fungal spores, viruses, or bacteria. Air-borne particulate matter, such as asbestos fibers or smoke particles, can also be found in air and be inhaled. Other significant and toxic pollutants include gases such as ozone and carbon monoxide, as well as poisonous compounds such as lead.

The U.S. Environmental Protection Agency (EPA) helped to establish the Clean Air Act in 1970 as a means of setting and achieving air quality standards for the United States. Since the law was enacted, the EPA has been steadily monitoring air quality and charting our progress toward meeting the goals of this important act (Figure 2.2). Although its primary focus has been the quality of outdoor air, the EPA, along with the American Lung Association, has more recently been involved with assessing the impact of indoor air pollution on human health.

In 2002, the EPA reported that during the previous 20 years, the United States reduced the emissions of five out of six major air pollutants: lead, ozone, carbon monoxide, particulate matter, and sulfur dioxide. However, emissions of the nitrogen oxides increased during that same period. Despite this progress, the EPA reports that in the United States alone, more than 160,000,000 tons of pollutants were released into the air in 2000. In addition, more than 121,000,000 people lived in counties that did not meet the air quality standards for at least one of these major pollutants.

Inhaling these pollutants can seriously affect an individual's health. Lead accumulates in our blood, bones, and other tissues and interferes with the normal functioning of important organs such as the brain, kidney, and liver. The reduction in lead emissions, a direct result of moving to unleaded gasoline, is seen as one of the major successes of the Clean Air Act legislation. Lead levels in 2000 were 93% lower than the levels detected in 1981. Chronic exposure to ozone may permanently damage the lungs and may worsen such health problems as bronchitis, emphysema, asthma, and heart disease. Particulate matter in the air can reduce lung function and, like ozone, promote a wide variety of respiratory diseases. Carbon monoxide reduces oxygen delivery to all of the body's tissues and, for this reason, is very poisonous at high levels. When asthmatic individuals are exposed to sulfur dioxide, they will often experience shortness of breath and wheezing. Long-term exposure to nitrogen dioxide, one of the more common nitrogen oxides, can permanently alter the lung tissue and increase vulnerability to lung infections.

Health officials are particularly concerned about the impact of outdoor pollution on children because they are at a greater health risk when exposed to these airborne pollutants. Because they are more active outdoors and their lungs are still developing, they are more likely to sustain long-term damage to their respiratory systems.

As you learn more about your respiratory system and gain an understanding of the critical role it plays in sustaining life, it is likely that you will also come to appreciate the concerns of environmental health officials. By using chemicals and polluting our atmosphere, people are putting their health and quality of life at risk.

Because atmospheric gas is a mixture of individual gases such as oxygen and nitrogen, the sum of all the partial pressures of the individual gases in the atmosphere is called the **total atmospheric pressure** or the **barometric pressure**. The total atmospheric pressure varies in different regions of the world as a result of differences in altitude and local weather conditions.

At sea level, the total atmospheric pressure is 760 mm Hg. Because 21% of the gas molecules in a given volume of air at sea level are oxygen molecules, the pressure that the oxygen molecules contribute to the total pressure at sea level can be calculated using the following method: multiply 760 mm Hg

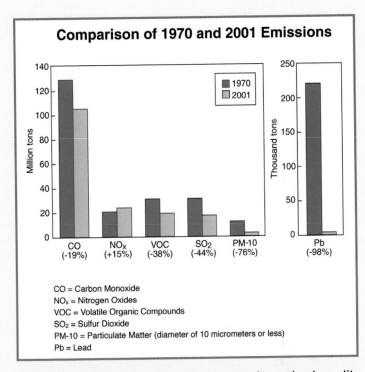

Figure 2.2 This graph shows the percent change in air quality in the United States during the past two decades. A negative value indicates a reduction in the emission of that pollutant during the time period. A positive value indicates an increase in the rate of emission. The six pollutants listed were set as the standard indicators of air quality by the EPA.

by 0.21 (or 21%). Thus, the partial pressure for oxygen (or PO_2) is 160 mm Hg.

The density of the atmosphere decreases with increasing altitude (Figure 2.3). As a result, the total atmospheric pressure on the top of Mount Everest is about 250 mm Hg, so the partial pressure of oxygen would equal 53 mm Hg. The availability of oxygen, as measured by partial pressure, is much lower on Mount Everest (53 mm Hg) than it is at sea level (160 mm Hg).

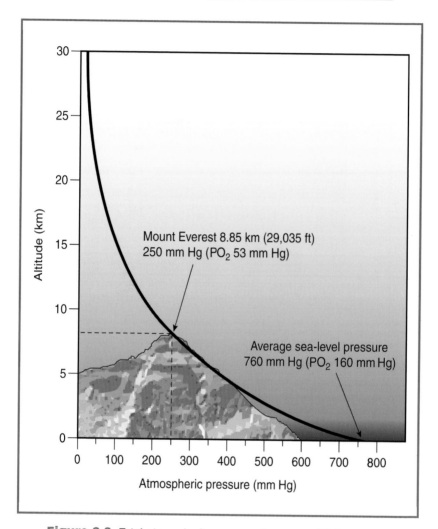

Figure 2.3 Total atmospheric pressure decreases with increasing altitude, affecting the partial pressures of the individual gases in the atmosphere. This concept is illustrated here. The PO_2 at sea level is significantly higher than the PO_2 at the top of Mount Everest.

Later chapters focus on the transport and fate of the two atmospheric gas molecules considered to be of great physiological importance: oxygen (O_2) and carbon dioxide (CO_2). First, we will discuss how the body uses oxygen.

CONNECTIONS

Earth's atmosphere consists primarily of nitrogen (about 79%) and oxygen (21%) along with small amounts of argon, neon, carbon dioxide, and variable amounts of water vapor. Oxygen and carbon dioxide are the physiologically relevant gases in the atmosphere. The appropriate measure of the availability of oxygen, for respiration or other functions, is its partial pressure, which is directly proportional to its concentration. The composition of Earth's atmosphere has changed over time, and human activities now threaten the quality of the air.

3

Why Do We Breathe?

Humans and other mammals will die if deprived of oxygen. In humans, irreversible damage to the brain can occur within minutes of losing its oxygen supply. Although some cells are more sensitive to oxygen deprivation than others, all human tissues require oxygen and eventually die without it. This chapter will address why cells need oxygen to function and survive.

CELLULAR RESPIRATION

Oxygen is required for the process called **cellular respiration** (also known as cellular metabolism). This process should not be confused with the larger-scale process of respiration on which this book is based. Cellular respiration is the process by which complex energy-bearing food molecules, like glucose ($C_6H_{12}O_6$) and fatty acids, are broken down to the much simpler molecules of carbon dioxide (CO_2) and water (H_2O) to make energy in the form of **adenosine triphosphate**, or **ATP** (Figure 3.1).

Cellular respiration requires several steps to break down food molecules, such as glucose, and generate ATP (Figure 3.2), the useful form of cellular energy. In these steps, high-energy electrons in the food molecules are systematically removed and transferred from one electron acceptor to another. The final electron acceptor in this long series of electron transfer steps is oxygen. Once oxygen accepts these electrons, it is converted to

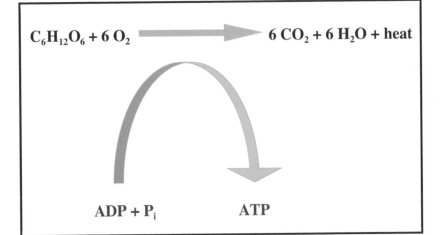

Figure 3.1 The overall chemical reaction for the process of cellular respiration is diagrammed here. In the presence of O_2, energy-bearing food molecules (represented here by glucose, or $C_6H_{12}O_6$) are broken down to produce ATP, the useful form of cellular energy. As a result, the "waste" products of carbon dioxide (CO_2), water (H_2O), and heat are formed. During the process, a molecule of ADP (adenosine diphosphate) combines with a free phosphate atom (P_i) to form ATP.

water, one of the "waste" products of cellular respiration (refer again to Figure 3.1).

If oxygen is absent and unable to serve as the final electron acceptor, then all of the preceding electron transfer steps will be interrupted and ATP production will be halted. The lack of ATP will prevent cells from doing their work, cellular processes will begin to shut down, and cells will eventually die. Therefore, one of the primary functions of the respiratory system is to provide oxygen to cells so the cells can make ATP and perform their various functions.

MEASURING METABOLIC RATE AND OXYGEN DEMAND

What is metabolism? When we describe our metabolism, we are actually referring to our overall rate of cellular respiration, or metabolic rate. The metabolic rate is the sum of all the individual rates of cellular respiration occurring

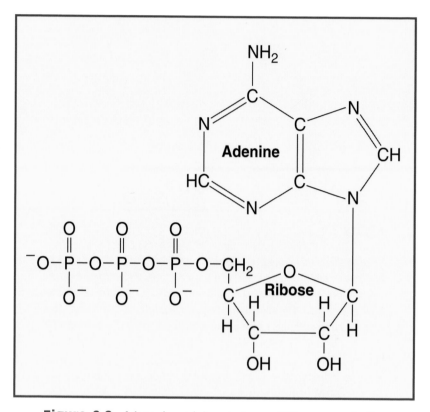

Figure 3.2 Adenosine triphosphate, or ATP, represents the form of energy that cells use to do work. Cellular work includes such activities as transportation of substances, synthesis of new products, and muscular contraction. The chemical structure of ATP is illustrated here.

within the various tissues at any one time and under specified circumstances.

In theory, there are a variety of potential indicators of metabolic rate. For example, the rate at which food (energy) is consumed could be measured. Alternatively, the rate of O_2 consumption, the rate of CO_2 production, the rate of H_2O production, the rate of ATP production, or the rate of heat production could be measured. All of these factors reflect the overall rate of cellular respiration.

However, some of these potential measures are more reliable and more practical to obtain than others. Because the amount of oxygen consumed is directly proportional to the rate of cellular respiration, measuring the amount of oxygen consumed is the most common method used to assess metabolic rate. This method can be used to indirectly measure the rate of energy consumption under a variety of conditions. The **basal metabolic rate**, or **BMR**, is a measure of the rate of energy consumption under basal conditions; that is, while a person is at rest, awake, and fasting in a temperature-controlled environment.

Although it would seem that the rate of oxygen consumption under basal conditions would be quite low, maintaining the basal metabolic rate typically represents the greatest energy expenditure, and therefore the greatest need for oxygen, for the body on a daily basis. This is because the BMR represents the total amount of energy required over a given time period to support the activities of the brain, kidneys, heart, lungs, liver, and other metabolically active organs.

Physiologists have found that humans vary widely with respect to their individual basal metabolic rates. Factors such as sex, body size, body temperature, and endocrine status can affect BMR. For example, when comparing two individuals of similar size, a male will have a higher BMR than a female. A smaller individual will have a higher BMR per kilogram of body weight than a larger individual. Smaller individuals lose body heat more rapidly than larger individuals and, as a consequence, expend more energy maintaining body temperature at 37° C (98.6° F).

A highly trained athlete will exhibit an overall higher basal metabolic rate when compared to another individual of similar weight and size who is not athletic. As a consequence, the athlete will consume more oxygen per unit of time. A growing child or a pregnant woman consumes more oxygen per unit of body weight (per kg) than the average adult because they are actively synthesizing new body tissues.

Oxygen consumption rates have also been used as an indirect measure of the energetic costs of non-basal activities, such as sitting or running. When a person is running, for example, some of the oxygen he or she is consuming is still being directed to the basal activities described previously, while an additional amount is being consumed to support the activity. By placing a mask over a person running on a treadmill, a respiratory gas analyzer can regulate the oxygen level of the air being inhaled while monitoring the O_2 and CO_2 levels of the expired air (Figure 3.3). Experiments such as these have provided the energy expenditures associated with the various activities listed in Figure 3.4 on page 28.

As a consequence, the oxygen needs of any given individual can vary during the course of a day. A person consumes less oxygen per hour while sleeping than while driving a car. A person consumes less oxygen per hour driving a car than while running. Later in this book, we will explore how the respiratory system adjusts to meet changing demands for oxygen.

Certain human tissues have greater oxygen demands than others. The circulatory system accommodates this need by sending a greater portion of the blood supply to the more metabolically active organs. Those tissues with a high rate of oxygen consumption, such as the brain, are more sensitive to periods of oxygen deprivation.

In human muscle tissue, temporary deficits in oxygen are tolerated during periods of intense muscle activity due to the presence of an anaerobic (no oxygen required) metabolic pathway called **lactic acid fermentation.** When the demand for ATP exceeds the body's ability to supply O_2 to the muscles, lactic acid fermentation provides an additional source of ATP to support muscular work. Supplemental anaerobic ATP production comes with a cost, however. A byproduct of this pathway is lactic acid, which causes muscle soreness and promotes muscle fatigue.

In conclusion, humans exhibit a wide range of metabolic rates and, hence, have varied needs for oxygen.

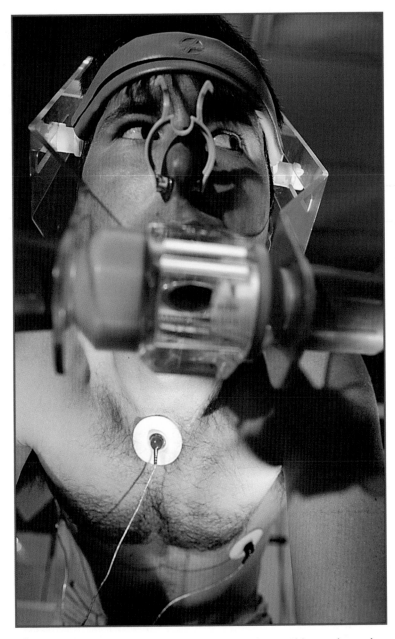

Figure 3.3 Respiratory gas analyzers, such as the one this man is wearing, can be used to monitor the O_2 consumption rates of humans engaged in activities such as exercise.

ENERGY EXPENDITURE DURING DIFFERENT TYPES OF ACTIVITY FOR A 154-LB PERSON

FORM OF ACTIVITY	ENERGY KCAL/H
LYING STILL, AWAKE	77
SITTING AT REST	100
TYPEWRITING RAPIDLY	140
DRESSING OR UNDRESSING	150
WALKING ON LEVEL, 4.3 KM/H (2.6 MI/H)	200
BICYCLING ON LEVEL, 9 KM/H (5.5 MI/H)	304
WALKING ON 3 PERCENT GRADE, 4.3 KM/H (2.6 MI/H)	357
SAWING WOOD OR SHOVELING SNOW	480
JOGGING, 9 KM/H (5.3 MI/H)	570
ROWING, 20 STROKES/MIN	828

Figure 3.4 The amount of energy expended (in kilocalories per hour) for various activities is listed in this table. Values are based on those of a 70-kg (or 154-lb) person.

CONNECTIONS

Overall, humans require a constant and ample supply of ATP. For cells to produce large amounts of ATP using the process of cellular respiration, they also need a constant and ample supply of oxygen. The next chapter will discuss how the human respiratory system is well-designed to meet the body's oxygen demands.

4

Anatomy of the Respiratory System

The function of an organ is reflected in its structure, and the human lung is no exception. A reasonable analogy for the design of the human respiratory system is an upside-down tree (Figure 4.1). As one goes from the base of the tree to its top, larger branches continue to split off into smaller branches. Similarly, larger airways branch off into smaller airways until the surface of the lung is reached. The human respiratory system can be divided into three main regions based on function. Much of the respiratory system consists of an upper tract of structures with diverse functions that lead to a lower tract of branching airways designed to deliver air to the alveoli. The alveoli, located at the lung surface, are the site of gas exchange between the air and blood.

THE UPPER RESPIRATORY TRACT

The nose, nasal cavity, sinuses, and pharynx are all organs of the upper respiratory tract (Figure 4.2). When a person breathes in through the **nose**, air is directed through the two nostrils and into the divided **nasal cavity**, a hollow space behind the nose. The nostrils contain numerous hairs that prevent large particles from being inhaled. The nasal cavity is lined with a mucous membrane and has a rich blood supply. The mucus produced by the **goblet cells** of the membrane traps smaller particles entering with the air. The epithelial cells lining the nasal cavity have tiny hair-like projections called cilia

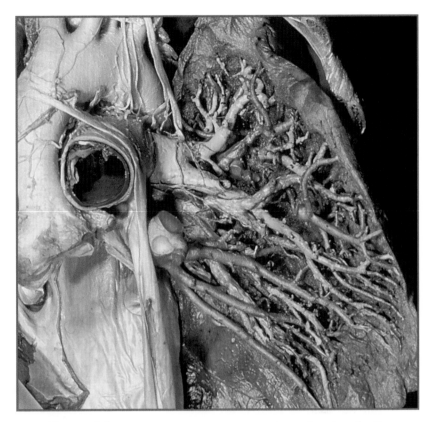

Figure 4.1 An upside-down tree represents a good analogy for the overall structure of the highly branched human respiratory system. This can be seen in the model of a human lung, shown here.

that move the particle-laden mucus downward in the direction of the pharynx, or throat, where it is swallowed.

The nasal cavity serves to warm and humidify the air before it heads to the lungs. It can also recapture some of that heat and moisture as the air is exhaled through the nose, but not the mouth. For this reason, breathing through the mouth increases the rate of water and heat loss associated with the process of respiration.

We are aware that the nose and nasal cavities are involved in the sense of smell, otherwise known as olfaction, a form of chemoreception (further discussed in Chapter 8). The binding of airborne molecules to the olfactory cells, specialized receptor

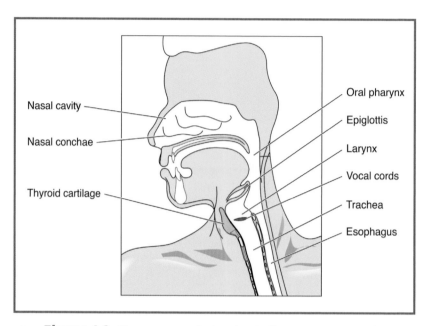

Figure 4.2 **The upper respiratory tract allows a person to take air into his or her body.**

cells located in a particular region of the nasal cavity, allows humans to detect over 200 different odors. The chemical nature of the odor can help protect us from breathing in a noxious chemical or can help us to locate a food source (or, perhaps, even a suitable mate).

The nasal cavity is surrounded by **sinuses**, which are thought to lighten the skull, help warm and moisten the air inhaled, and act as resonance chambers for speech. Many of us are aware that we possess sinuses, if only because they have caused us discomfort in the form of headaches or infections. The mucous membranes lining the sinus cavities are continuous with those lining the nasal cavity. Mucus produced in the sinuses drains into the nasal cavity. A sinus headache can occur when the passages into the nasal cavity are blocked by inflamed tissue, thus preventing drainage and leading to a buildup of pressure.

We can breathe through both our mouths and nasal passages. In either case, air from the mouth and the nasal passages is directed into the **pharynx**, or throat, a structure that connects both to the **larynx**, which leads into the **trachea**, or windpipe (for the passage of air), and to the **esophagus** (for passage of food and water). The larynx prevents foreign objects from entering the trachea and lower respiratory tract. Among other structures, the larynx contains the **vocal cords**, two muscular folds that vibrate as air passes through, producing sound. Tightening the vocal cords results in a higher pitched sound, while low-pitched sounds are generated when the cords are relaxed. The pharynx, which lies above the larynx, also contributes to the production of speech.

THE LOWER RESPIRATORY TRACT

Before we examine the structure and function of the trachea and the other conducting airways that deliver air to the surface of the lungs, let's explore some of the features they share in common. Like the nasal and sinus cavities, the epithelial lining of the trachea possesses mucus-producing goblet cells. The mucus functions in a similar fashion to trap small airborne particles. The ciliated epithelial cells move the mucus upward to the pharynx, where it is swallowed and digested within the stomach.

The mucus produced in the airways is dense and sticky, and typically floats on the surface of the epithelium on a thin layer of watery fluid. Individuals who suffer from the genetic disorder known as **cystic fibrosis** have faulty chloride ion channels and cannot manufacture the watery fluid. As a consequence, the thick, sticky mucus adheres to the linings of their airways, interfering with airflow to the lung surface and providing a breeding ground for bacterial infection (Figure 4.3).

The trachea (Figure 4.4) is the main passage to the lungs and lies in front of the muscular esophagus. In the upper chest

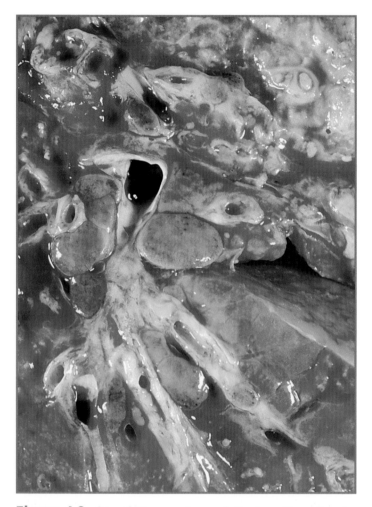

Figure 4.3 One of the symptoms of the hereditary disorder cystic fibrosis is the production of thick, sticky mucus that clogs the airways and provides a breeding ground for bacteria. A photograph of a lung from an individual with cystic fibrosis is shown here. Notice the excessive amount of mucus coating the airways.

region, the trachea splits into the right and left bronchi that supply air to the right and left lung, respectively. The opening to the trachea is covered by a small flap of tissue called the **epiglottis**, which prevents food and liquids from entering the trachea.

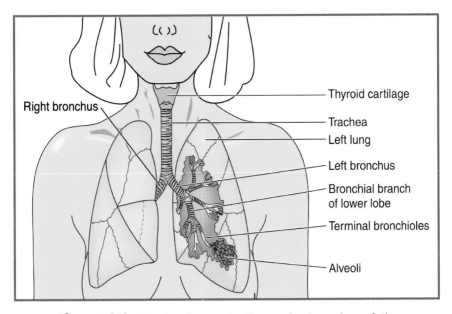

Right bronchus

Thyroid cartilage

Trachea

Left lung

Left bronchus

Bronchial branch
of lower lobe

Terminal bronchioles

Alveoli

Figure 4.4 **The trachea and other major branches of the conducting airways are illustrated here. The cartilaginous rings around the trachea provide rigidity and prevent its collapse. The major branches include the left and right bronchus (right bronchus not shown), the terminal bronchioles, and the alveoli.**

Rings of cartilage prevent the trachea from collapsing, keeping this important airway open. You can feel these rings by probing the front of your neck with your fingertips. The tracheal rings are C-shaped to allow for the expansion of the esophagus when we swallow food. Smooth muscle and connective tissue connect these rings to complete the tubular shape of the trachea and allow for some flexibility.

Air passing through the trachea next enters the bronchial tree, a series of branching tubes of progressively smaller diameter that lead to the lung surface. Before examining the characteristics of some of these branches, it is important to recognize that gas exchange only occurs at the lung surface. For this reason, the volume of air residing within all of these finely branched airways is known as the anatomical dead space. This air of the anatomical dead space does not reach the lung surface and does not contribute to the process of gas exchange with the blood. In fact, as you will learn in Chapter 6, the anatomical dead space has a significant effect on the PO_2 levels at the lung surface.

The largest of these bronchial branches, the right and left primary **bronchi** (*bronchus* is the singular), supply air to the right and left lungs, respectively. The primary bronchi are similar in structure to the trachea except that the supporting cartilage is plate-like rather than C-shaped.

Within a short distance, the left primary bronchus splits into two secondary bronchi, while the right primary bronchus splits into three secondary bronchi. The difference in the number of secondary bronchi can be attributed to the number of lobes that each lung has. The right lung is composed of three major lobes, while the left lung has only two to provide room for the heart, the other major organ found in the chest cavity.

In the 1960s, the Swiss anatomist Ewald Weibel undertook the painstaking task of determining how many times the typical airway branches before reaching the surface of the lung. He computed an average value of 16 times! The names and numbers of these branches at several levels are depicted in Figure 4.5. By the time the site of gas exchange is reached, the number of individual branches is about one-half million.

As the respiratory tubes branch into the tubes of smaller diameters known as the **bronchioles**, the cartilage plates seen in the bronchi, disappear altogether. At this level, the smooth muscle becomes more prominent. Elastic fibers embedded in these tubes of smooth muscle impart an elastic or "snap-back" property to lung tissue. The elastic properties of the lung help to expel deoxygenated air during exhalation. Changes also occur in the lining of the bronchioles as they become progressively smaller. The number of mucus-producing goblet cells decreases, the epithelial cells become more flattened, and there

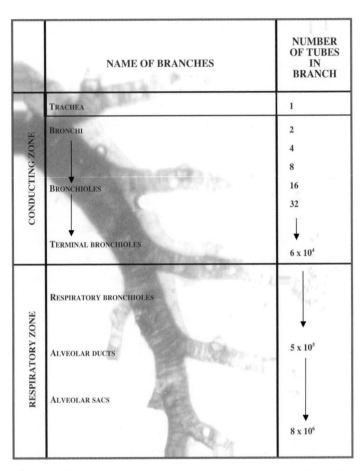

NAME OF BRANCHES	NUMBER OF TUBES IN BRANCH
TRACHEA	1
BRONCHI	2
	4
	8
BRONCHIOLES	16
	32
TERMINAL BRONCHIOLES	6×10^4
RESPIRATORY BRONCHIOLES	
ALVEOLAR DUCTS	5×10^5
ALVEOLAR SACS	
	8×10^6

Figure 4.5 A representation of the names and numbers of branches of the human respiratory system is illustrated here. The conducting zone represents the airways that deliver air to the respiratory zone. The respiratory zone represents sites where gas exchange with the blood can occur. Notice that as the branches get smaller, they are more numerous.

are fewer cilia. The mucus lining becomes very thin, until it disappears altogether.

These changes should not be surprising as we approach the region of the respiratory surface involved in gas exchange. As we will learn in the next chapter, Fick's law predicts that diffusion is enhanced when the diffusion distance, in this case the distance between air and blood, is short. A taller layer of mucus-producing and epithelial cells would reduce the rate of gas exchange.

THE LUNG SURFACE

The final series of bronchioles are the **respiratory bronchioles**. These branch off into **alveolar ducts**, which end in microscopic air pockets, or sacs, called **alveoli** (*alveolus* is the singular, Figure 4.6). The alveoli are the site for exchange of the respiratory gases, O_2 and CO_2, between the air and the blood. The outer surface of each air-filled alveolar sac is covered with pulmonary capillaries, the tiny vessels that will pick up O_2 and give off CO_2. It is estimated that the total alveolar surface for gas exchange in the human lung is equivalent to 70 square meters, or about one-half the size of a tennis court!

The walls of the alveoli (Figure 4.7) consist of a single layer of flattened squamous epithelial cells called **type I alveolar epithelial cells** that have a basement membrane. The outer surface of each air-filled alveolar sac is covered with pulmonary capillaries, tiny blood vessels, which consist of endothelial cells and their basement membrane. The epithelial cells of the alveoli and the endothelial cells of the capillaries are surrounded by interstitium, or fluid. Together, the walls of the alveoli and capillaries and their fused basement membranes make up the **respiratory membrane.**

The distance for diffusion between the air in the alveolus and the blood in the pulmonary capillary is very short. If we start on the inside of the alveolus, we can see that an oxygen molecule must first diffuse through a single layer of flattened alveolar epithelial cells and their supporting basement membrane. The O_2 molecule would then pass through the interstitium, the extracellular fluid surrounding cells, and finally through the wall of the pulmonary capillary, consisting of endothelial cells and their basement membrane, before it enters the blood. Conversely, a molecule of CO_2 would

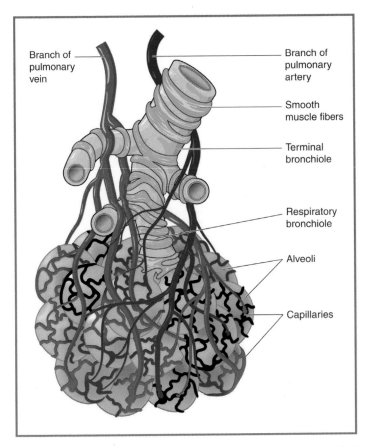

Branch of pulmonary vein

Branch of pulmonary artery

Smooth muscle fibers

Terminal bronchiole

Respiratory bronchiole

Alveoli

Capillaries

Figure 4.6 Respiratory bronchioles end in microscopic sacs called alveoli, the major site of gas exchange between the atmosphere and the blood. Note the close structural relationship between the blood vessels and the alveolar clusters. This promotes gas exchange between the lungs and the circulatory system.

pass through the pulmonary capillary wall, some interstitial fluid, and the alveolar membrane before reaching the air within the alveolus.

In addition to the type I cells, there are **type II alveolar epithelial cells**, which secrete a fluid containing surfactants and are also involved in gas exchange. The function of surfactants is described in Chapter 7. Immune cells known as

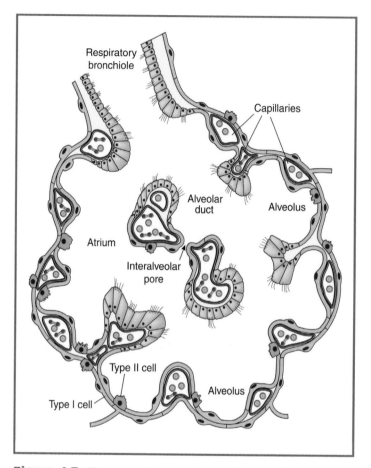

Figure 4.7 The respiratory membrane, through which gas must diffuse, consists of a single layer of flattened type I alveolar cells, interstitium, and the capillary endothelium or wall. Type II alveolar cells produce surfactant, while alveolar macrophages (not shown) prevent airborne infectious agents from entering the body.

macrophages can also be found in the alveoli and serve to keep them clean of airborne particles and bacteria.

THE PLEURA AND PLEURAL CAVITY

A thin membrane called the **pleura** attaches to and completely surrounds both lungs (Figure 4.8). The **visceral pleural**

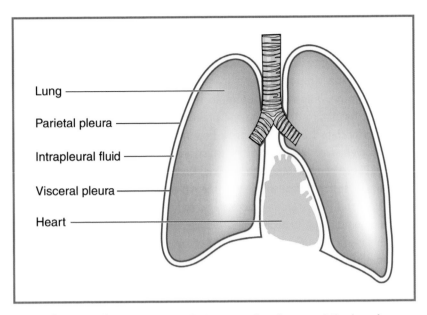

Lung

Parietal pleura

Intrapleural fluid

Visceral pleura

Heart

Figure 4.8 The relationship between the pleura and the lung is illustrated in this diagram. The parietal pleural membrane is in contact with the inner thoracic wall, while the visceral pleural membrane lines the outer surface of the lung. These two membranes are contiguous with each other and form a thin cavity that is filled with fluid.

membrane, in contact with the outer surface of the lung, is continuous with the **parietal pleural membrane** that lines the inner wall of the thoracic cavity. The very thin space lying between these two membranes is called the **pleural cavity**. The membranes secrete a lubricating fluid into this tiny space that helps to reduce tissue friction during breathing movements. The fluid also serves to keep the visceral and parietal membranes adhered to each other. The importance of this characteristic will become apparent in later chapters that address how we breathe.

CONNECTIONS
The many branches of conducting airways serve to maintain unrestricted airflow to the lung surface and to keep the lungs

VISUALIZING THE LUNGS

MRI (magnetic resonance imaging) and **PET (positron emission tomography)** scans have significantly advanced medicine, allowing doctors to produce detailed images of soft tissues to determine the presence of disease and to plan appropriate treatment. These new imaging technologies have supplemented the use of X-rays, which are limited to providing images of dense body tissues such as bone. Despite major advances in the ability to form clear images of internal organs through the use of MRI and PET scanning technology, some organs of the body still remain difficult to accurately visualize. Unfortunately, one of these organs is the lungs. The treatment of lung disease is hampered by the inability of physicians to obtain useful images.

It now appears, however, that another advance in medical imaging will greatly help to eliminate this problem. Researchers in the United States and Europe are now generating high-quality lung scans by having volunteers in their studies inhale specially treated gases. These gases contain unusual isotopes of helium or xenon that all orient in the same direction (or "hyperpolarize") when subjected to a magnetic field. Other hyperpolarized gas mixtures are being tested that make use of laser-treated rubidium atoms.

Individuals inhale the treated gas and hold their breath while they undergo an MRI scan. The signal that is generated with these treated gases is 100,000 times stronger than those usually produced. Using these gases during an MRI, physicians are able to detect specific regions of the lung affected by emphysema and chronic obstructive pulmonary diseases.

Clinical trials will begin as soon as concerns about any potential health effects of breathing these alternative gases are addressed. There is also additional research needed to optimize the imaging technology and medical protocols. This technology may also revolutionize the imaging of other organs, including the colon. Given the high incidence of colon cancer and the increased demand for colon cancer screening in the United States, the development of this new imaging technique represents an important medical advance.

clear of airborne particles and bacteria. The pleural membranes and cavity are important in reducing friction during breathing and in keeping the lung inflated.

The next chapter examines the transport process by which oxygen moves from the atmosphere into our tissues. The anatomical design of the respiratory system supports this function. At the site for gas exchange between the atmosphere and the blood, the lung tissue is composed of 500,000 alveolar sacs, which have a collective surface area for gas exchange of more than 70 square meters. The respiratory gases, CO_2 and O_2, diffuse over a very short distance through a thin respiratory membrane composed of the alveolar membrane, interstitium, and the capillary endothelium.

5

The Diffusion of Gas Molecules

In humans, the respiratory system works with the circulatory system to deliver oxygen, obtained from the atmosphere, to the tissues, where oxygen is needed for cellular respiration (Figure 5.1). The human respiratory system and circulatory system rely on a form of transport known as bulk flow to bring volumes of air (with O_2) into the lungs or volumes of blood (with O_2) to the tissues. How bulk movement is accomplished will be addressed in Chapter 6. For now, it is sufficient to know that bulk flow depends on differences in pressure and requires energy in the form of ATP.

At all other points in this oxygen delivery system, however, oxygen transport is dependent on a passive (no ATP required) form of transport known as diffusion. In this chapter, we will focus on the process of diffusion and examine how the use of this process impacts the design of the respiratory system.

DIFFUSION

Once atmospheric air has been brought to the surface of the lungs in very close proximity to the blood supply, oxygen molecules will move from the air into the blood. The form of transport used for this stage of oxygen transport is called diffusion. Diffusion is the process by which molecules spontaneously move from one region to another in a medium such as air or water. Above absolute zero temperature (0 Kelvin) all molecules possess kinetic energy and

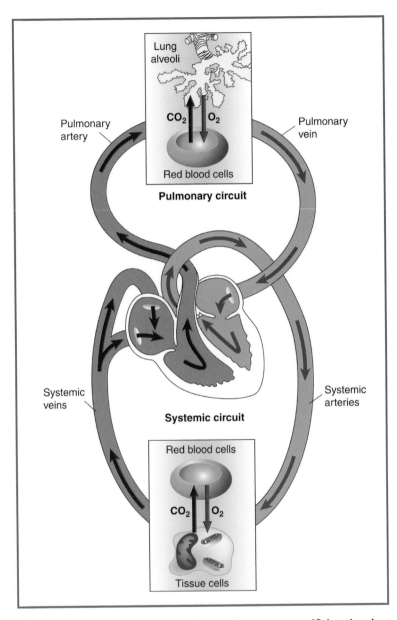

Figure 5.1 During the process of gas exchange, oxygen (O_2) and carbon dioxide (CO_2) are transferred between the lungs and the bloodstream. O_2-rich air is brought to the surface of the lung by bulk flow, but movement of O_2 into the blood occurs via diffusion. Likewise, O_2-rich blood is brought in close proximity to cells by bulk flow, but diffusion is the process that drives the O_2 movement from blood into mitochondria, where it is consumed by cellular respiration.

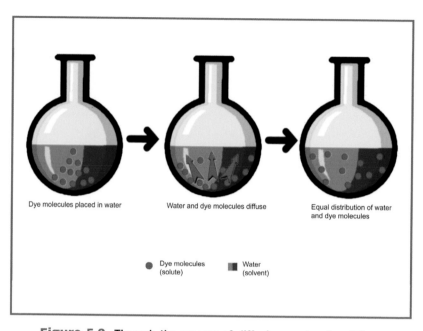

Dye molecules placed in water

Water and dye molecules diffuse

Equal distribution of water and dye molecules

● Dye molecules (solute)   ■ Water (solvent)

Figure 5.2 Through the process of diffusion, molecules diffuse across a permeable membrane from a region of higher concentration to lower concentration until equilibrium is established.

are in constant random motion. Molecules move and collide with other molecules and as the temperature of the medium increases, the rate of these random movements and resulting collisions also increases.

Diffusion is the net movement of molecules from a region of higher concentration to one of lower concentration (Figure 5.2). Once equilibrium has been achieved (i.e., once the concentrations of the molecule are the same in both regions), the rates of movement between the two regions are equal and the overall net rate of diffusion is zero.

FICK'S LAW

There are many factors that influence the rate at which molecules, such as oxygen, diffuse from one area to another. **Fick's law** describes the effects of these factors on the net rate

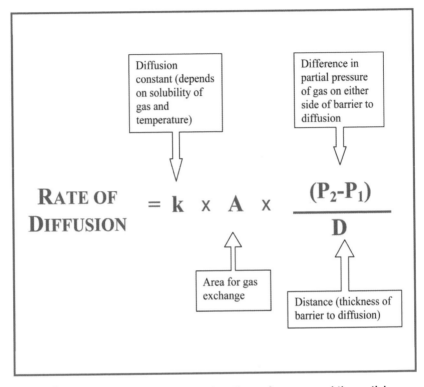

Figure 5.3 According to Fick's law, the surface area and the partial pressure gradient affect the rate of diffusion of oxygen from the atmosphere to the blood. As the surface area for exchange increases, the rate of diffusion increases. Similarly, an increase in the partial pressure gradient will also increase the rate of gas diffusion.

of diffusion of a molecule (Figure 5.3). Fick's law can be applied to the rate that oxygen diffuses from the atmosphere across the respiratory membrane and into the blood, and to the rate that carbon dioxide diffuses in the opposite direction.

According to Fick's law, an increase in the **surface area** for gas exchange (i.e., the surface area of the lung) will increase the rate of O_2 diffusion. An individual who has a portion of lung tissue damaged because of cancer, for example, has a reduced surface for gas exchange and, as a consequence, a reduced rate of O_2 uptake.

The **partial pressure gradient** (P_2-P_1) is the difference in partial pressures between the region with the higher PO_2 (or P_2) and that with the lower PO_2 (or P_1). The net diffusion of oxygen is always from the atmosphere (P_2) to the blood (P_1), because the PO_2 of the atmosphere is greater than the PO_2

NITROGEN AND DECOMPRESSION SICKNESS

The low atmospheric partial pressure of oxygen (PO_2) levels found in high-altitude environments help us to understand one of the important components of Fick's law, the partial pressure gradient. At a high altitude, low atmospheric PO_2 levels reduce the partial pressure gradient for O_2 uptake. In other words, if a person is at a high altitude such as Mount Everest, the total air pressure decreases from 760 mm Hg to 250 mm Hg, so the partial pressure of oxygen also decreases. The same principle holds true for when a person is under water.

Decompression sickness, commonly referred to as "the bends," is a condition that scuba divers have to be careful to avoid. As a diver descends to greater depths, the total water pressure increases. For example, at a depth of 33 feet, the total pressure doubles from 760 mm Hg at the surface to 1580 mm Hg. As a consequence, the partial pressures of the individual gases also increase.

Scuba divers typically breathe a mixture of 21% O_2 and 79% N_2, a composition that is similar to normal air. Therefore, as a diver descends, the partial pressure gradients for N_2 and O_2 increase and the PN_2 and PO_2 levels of the diver's blood rise to levels above those obtained at sea level. Although nitrogen gas is physiologically inert (inactive), levels in the blood continue to rise with increasing depth and duration of the dive.

At high blood levels, a state of confusion called nitrogen narcosis can occur. This condition can cause divers to become dizzy and giddy and act as if they were intoxicated. Nitrogen narcosis leaves no lasting effect on the body and is reversed as the pressure decreases (as the diver ascends).

of blood. If P_1 were equal to P_2 (or $P_2-P_1=0$), there would be no net rate of diffusion. For diffusion to occur, a difference must exist in the partial pressures between the two regions.

Several factors affect the rate of diffusion of oxygen into the lungs. As you read in Chapter 2, altitude affects the partial

A far more common and serious condition, decompression sickness, can occur as a diver with increased blood PN_2 levels returns to the surface too quickly. Decompression sickness can lead to permanent physical impairment. As a diver returns to the surface, the dissolved nitrogen begins to leave the blood and tissues as the direction of the partial pressure gradient for nitrogen diffusion is reversed. If the ascent to the surface is too rapid, the diffusing nitrogen gas coalesces into bubbles that can cause pain and tissue damage. Normally, the bubbles of nitrogen will travel in the blood to the lungs, where they get trapped in the small pulmonary capillaries that surround the alveoli. The nitrogen bubbles eventually disappear as the diver exhales them.

In some cases, however, the bubbles travel to and get trapped in the capillaries supplying other tissues, reducing the flow of blood and oxygen to that region. If, for example, the capillaries to a joint are blocked, the diver will experience severe joint pain. Blockage of capillaries supplying nervous tissue can lead to a stroke or paralysis.

Divers learn to avoid this condition by conducting careful ascents to the surface and allowing adequate time for the nitrogen to leave the blood and tissues, thus avoiding bubble formation. Treatment for decompression sickness consists of quickly transferring the patient to a hyperbaric chamber to be recompressed. The high pressure in the chamber forces the nitrogen bubbles to grow smaller. The patient is then treated to a controlled gradual return to normal barometric pressure. Delay in the treatment may result in permanent paralysis due to nerve damage.

pressure of oxygen in the air. Fick's law allows us to quantify the impact of high altitude, which has reduced atmospheric PO_2, on O_2 uptake by the body. For example, at sea level, the partial pressure gradient for O_2 diffusion into the blood may be 160–40, or 120 mm Hg. At the top of Mount Everest, however, the gradient may be reduced to 53–40, or 13 mm Hg. This large drop in the partial pressure gradient greatly reduces the rate at which oxygen enters the blood. As you will learn later, the effect of the anatomy of the human respiratory system on actual lung PO_2 levels affects actual partial pressure gradients across the respiratory membrane. Blood PO_2 levels will also fall well below 40 mm Hg when O_2 availability is reduced.

Another factor that affects the diffusion rate is the thickness of the diffusion barrier, in this case, the respiratory membrane. If this barrier increases in thickness, the rate of diffusion will decrease.

Pulmonary edema is a condition in which fluid collects in the interstitium of the respiratory membrane, increasing the distance that oxygen molecules must diffuse to reach the blood (Figure 5.4). Individuals suffering from pulmonary edema cannot take up oxygen from the atmosphere as efficiently. One means of helping to counteract the reduced rate of diffusion is to increase the partial pressure gradient by providing the patient with pure oxygen to breathe, effectively increasing PO_2 levels from 160 to 760 mm Hg.

Diffusion is also temperature dependent. Because humans maintain a constant body temperature of 37° C (98.6° F), however, diffusion at the lung surface is always at that temperature.

CONNECTIONS

Chapter 5 described how Fick's law governs the rate of diffusion of molecules like oxygen and carbon dioxide, the respiratory gases. Based on the principles described in Fick's law, we might predict that a respiratory system would possess the following key features: (1) a large surface area for gas exchange, (2) a short

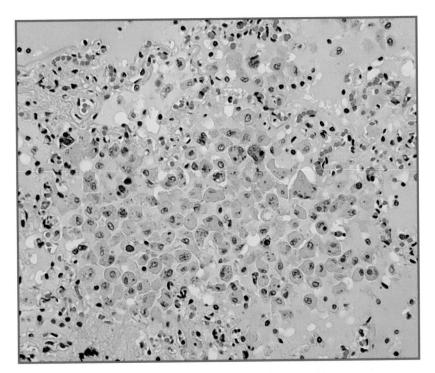

Figure 5.4 Breathing pure oxygen increases the partial pressure gradient for oxygen and can help to compensate for the effect pulmonary edema, a condition in which the thickness of the respiratory barrier (D) is increased. The photograph shows a section of a lung from a patient with pulmonary edema.

distance for oxygen diffusion, and (3) a design that maximizes the partial pressure gradient. Because humans have high metabolic rates and, therefore, high requirements for oxygen, we would expect the human respiratory system to incorporate these key design features in order to maximize the rate of oxygen uptake from the atmosphere. Thinking back to Chapter 4, where the anatomical design of the respiratory system was described, we find that our predictions hold true. The human respiratory system has both an extensive surface area for gas exchange (70 square meters) and an extremely thin barrier to gas diffusion in the alveoli.

6

How Do
We Breathe?

Much of the respiratory system consists of conducting airways like the trachea, bronchi, and bronchioles, structures designed to deliver air to the alveoli, where exchange of the gases O_2 and CO_2 with the blood occurs. The passive transport of molecules was discussed in the previous chapter. In this chapter, the bulk flow of air from the atmosphere to the alveoli and back out again will be discussed in more detail.

BOYLE'S LAW AND THE BULK FLOW OF AIR
In Chapter 4, it was stated that air moved in and out of the lungs by a transport process known as **bulk flow**. Bulk flow of a fluid-like substance (such as air, water, or blood) is achieved when pressure differences exist between two regions. Fluids will always flow from a high-pressure to a low-pressure region. For example, because blood pressure is higher in the arteries, blood always flows from the arteries toward the veins, where blood pressure is much lower. Differences in atmospheric pressure cause air to flow from one region of the atmosphere to another, creating wind.

Likewise, **inspiration**, also referred to as inhalation, or the bringing of air into the lungs, is achieved when air pressure in the lung is lower than air pressure in the surrounding atmosphere. When a person inhales, air moves from a region of higher pressure, the atmosphere, into the region of lower pressure, the lung. On the other

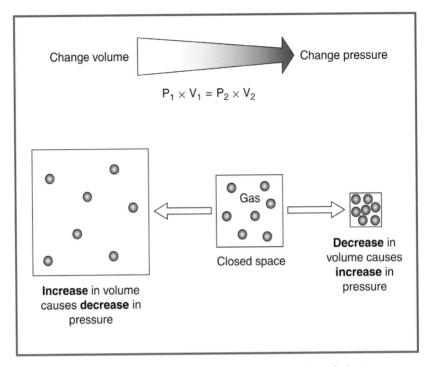

Change volume ━━━━━━━━━━▶ Change pressure

$$P_1 \times V_1 = P_2 \times V_2$$

Gas

Closed space

Increase in volume causes **decrease** in pressure

Decrease in volume causes **increase** in pressure

Figure 6.1 Boyle's law describes the inverse relationship between the pressure exerted by a constant number of gas molecules and the volume those gas molecules occupy. An increase in the volume of a gas will cause a decrease in its pressure.

hand, **expiration** or exhalation, the process of air moving out of the lungs, occurs when air pressure in the lungs is greater than atmospheric air pressure. Air will continue to flow either in or out of the lungs until air pressure in the lungs equals atmospheric pressure, or stated another way, until equilibrium with regard to air pressure is reached.

To understand how the differences in air pressure are created within the lung, it is important to understand **Boyle's law**. Boyle's law describes the relationship between a volume of gas and its pressure. For example, if there is a container filled with gas and the volume of the container increases, the pressure of the gas will decrease correspondingly. If the volume of the container of gas decreases, the pressure of the gas in the container will increase. Figure 6.1 illustrates

Boyle's law in both mathematical and schematic form. If the volume (V) of a gas is doubled, the pressure (P) is cut in half. If the volume of a gas is decreased to half its original volume, the pressure of the gas will double.

To take a breath, humans create a lower pressure in their lungs so that air will move in from the atmosphere. According to Boyle's law, to lower the air pressure in the lungs, the volume of the lungs must first be increased. An increase in the volume of the lungs will create a region of lower pressure and air will rush in from the atmosphere. Conversely, to move air out of our lungs or exhale, lung volume is decreased, causing the air pressure in the lung to increase. Air will flow out of the lungs into the atmosphere until lung pressure equals atmospheric pressure.

To take a breath, the lung volume must first increase, and to breathe out, lung volume must decrease. These changes in lung volume create pressure differences that cause airflow to occur. The muscles involved in changing lung volume are the **diaphragm** and the **intercostals**, or rib muscles (Figure 6.2).

The diaphragm is a sheet-like muscle that separates the thoracic cavity, containing the lungs and heart, from the abdominal cavity, where the organs of digestion, kidneys, liver, and spleen are located. Because the thoracic cavity is a separate compartment and lung tissue is so thin and elastic, changes in the volume of the thoracic cavity affect the volume of the lung.

When the diaphragm and external intercostals receive a stimulatory signal from the respiratory control center in the brainstem, they contract. The contraction of the diaphragm causes it to straighten and push down on the abdominal cavity and its contents. The contraction of the external intercostals causes the rib cage to expand upward and outward. Both the actions of the diaphragm and the rib muscles lead to increased lung volume and therefore decreased lung

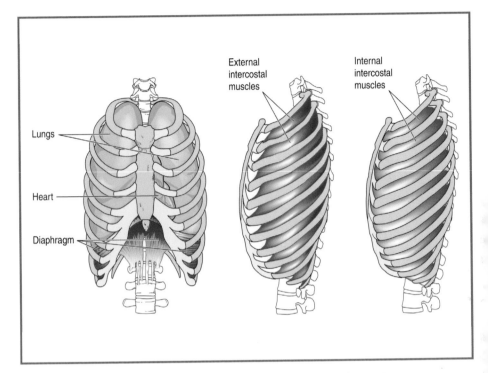

Lungs

Heart

Diaphragm

External intercostal muscles

Internal intercostal muscles

Figure 6.2 The respiratory muscles involved in changing lung volume and pressure are shown here. During quiet breathing, contraction of the diaphragm and external intercostals allows for inhalation, while relaxation of these muscles causes exhalation. Contraction of the internal intercostals promotes exhalation during exercise.

pressure (Figure 6.3 on left). Because expanding the lung volume to take in a breath of air requires muscular contraction, inspiration is an active process. Active processes require energy in the form of ATP.

In contrast, expiration is typically a passive process because it involves relaxation of the diaphragm and external intercostals. Once air pressure in the lungs is equivalent to atmospheric air pressure, airflow into the lungs stops. The relaxation of the diaphragm and external intercostals causes them to return to their original relaxed shape, decreasing the

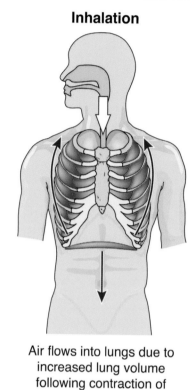

Inhalation

Exhalation

Air flows into lungs due to increased lung volume following contraction of diaphragm and external intercostal muscles

Air expelled from lungs due to relaxation of diaphragm and external intercostal muscles

Figure 6.3 During quiet breathing, contraction of the diaphragm and external intercostals increases lung volume (left). The lowered pressure allows air to move into the lung from the atmosphere. Relaxation of the diaphragm and external intercostals reduces lung volume (right) and air flows out of the lungs.

volume of the lung. As a result, the air within the lungs is pressurized and air flows out of the lung (Figure 6.3 on right). In addition, the elastic or "bounce-back" properties of the chest wall and lung tissue help these structures to return to their resting state.

Expiration can, however, become an active, energy-requiring

process. A set of rib muscles called the internal intercostals (refer again to Figure 6.2) will cause the chest cavity volume to decrease if activated, leading to a further increase in the air pressure in the lungs and causing a greater volume of air to be exhaled. The internal intercostals are often stimulated to contract during exercise, when oxygen needs are high, thus providing a greater volume of air exchanged with every breath and allowing for more rapid exchange of gases between the blood and the atmosphere. In a healthy individual under restful conditions, however, expiration is a passive process.

The **Heimlich maneuver** takes advantage of Boyle's law to remove foreign objects blocking the airway. As you will learn later in this chapter, even after a forceful exhalation, there is still quite a significant amount of air remaining in the lungs. If that remaining air were compressed to increase its pressure, it could dislodge the foreign object and open the airway. With the Heimlich maneuver, air compression is achieved by applying a vigorous upward thrust against the diaphragm, forcing the air into the thoracic cavity.

LUNG VOLUMES

Up to a certain point, humans are able to stimulate further expansion of the thoracic cavity through increased contraction of the diaphragm and external intercostals, thus creating even lower lung pressures relative to atmospheric pressure. This action allows a greater volume of air to enter the lungs. Conversely, humans are capable of expelling a greater amount of air from their lungs by forcing the thoracic cavity volume to relax beyond its normal resting state.

Terms have been developed to describe the various lung volumes associated with breathing and are useful in understanding the mechanics of breathing. The actual amounts (in liters) of these air volumes differ among humans and are determined for an individual through the use of an instrument

Figure 6.4 The woman in this picture is using a spirometer, which allows respiratory physiologists to determine the major respiratory volumes for an individual and to assess his or her respiratory function.

called a **spirometer**, typically used for assessing respiratory health and disease (Figure 6.4). It is designed to measure four different respiratory volumes.

The **tidal volume** is the amount of air an individual

takes in during normal, restful breathing (which also happens to equal to the volume of air exhaled during normal, restful breathing). As shown in the sample spirometer recording (Figure 6.5A), the tidal volume is usually about 0.5 or ½ liters. Notice that before taking a breath, the lungs still contain a considerable amount of air, approximately 2.3 liters. After taking a quiet breath, lung volume increases to 2.8 liters (therefore, the tidal volume = 2.8 – 2.3, or 0.5 liters).

The 2.3 liters of air remaining in the lungs after a normal exhalation can be divided into two important volumes: the **expiratory reserve volume** and the **residual volume**. To obtain these two volumes, the individual is asked to exhale forcibly and maximally immediately following a quiet exhalation. The quantity of air forced out of the lungs in this manner, typically 1.1 liters, is called the expiratory reserve volume. The air still remaining in the lung after that maneuver is called the residual volume. The residual volume of the lung is about 1.2 liters and helps to prevent our lungs from collapsing (Figure 6.5B).

The fourth important respiratory volume to be determined with the aid of the spirometer is the **inspiratory reserve volume**. To obtain this volume, the subject is asked just after taking a normal, restful breath to perform a forced, maximal inspiration (i.e., take as much air as possible into the lungs). In healthy adults, the inspiratory reserve volume is about 3 liters, or 6 times the amount of air inhaled during quiet breathing (Figure 6.5C).

To obtain the **total lung capacity**, all four of the respiratory volumes can be added together: the residual volume, the expiratory reserve volume, the tidal volume, and the inspiratory reserve volume. The total lung capacity for most healthy adults is close to 6 liters (Figure 6.5C). These respiratory volumes, along with other measures performed by the spirometer, can help medical professionals identify specific types of respiratory illnesses.

(Continued on page 64)

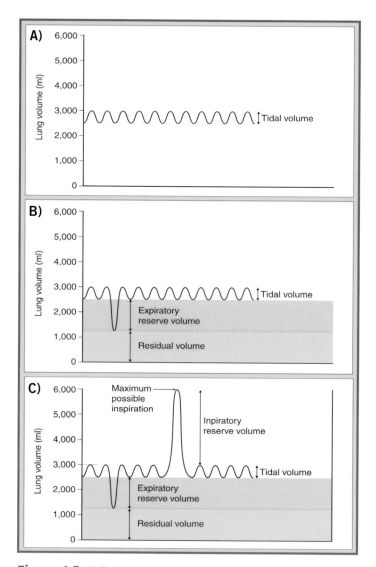

Figure 6.5 A) The tidal volume, typically 0.5 liters (500 ml), is the amount of air inhaled and exhaled during normal, restful breathing. **B)** The expiratory reserve volume is the maximum amount of air an individual can force from the lungs following a quiet expiration. The amount of air remaining in the lungs after exhaling is called the residual volume. **C)** The inspiratory reserve volume is the maximum amount of air an individual can take into the lungs following a quiet inspiration. The sum of all four volumes represents an individual's total lung capacity.

THE IRON LUNG AND
THE POLIO EPIDEMIC

The first recorded case of polio in the United States occurred in Vermont in 1894. However, it is believed that the polio virus inflicted children since at least 1500 B.C., as indicated on stone carvings in Egypt that depict children with obvious signs of the crippling disease. After 1894, there were a number of widespread outbreaks in the United States.

Until 1955, when a polio vaccine became available, paralytic poliomyelitis, or polio, was one of the most dreaded diseases in the United States and Canada. Summer was known as "polio season," and parents restricted their children's activities, particularly swimming, for fear their youngsters would catch this virus.

Polio victims suffered muscle paralysis. The polio virus, which is found in soil and water and is transmitted through feces, attacks the nerves of the spinal cord. The extent of paralysis depends on which nerves in the spinal cord are destroyed. If only the nerves in the lower portion of the spinal cord are infected, then the legs will become paralyzed. In more severe cases, the virus destroys the nerves in upper regions of the spinal cord and more extensive paralysis can occur.

One of the most famous victims of one of the polio epidemics that swept the United States was Franklin Delano Roosevelt, who later became president of the United States. Roosevelt caught polio in 1921, and his legs became permanently paralyzed. Despite being confined to a wheelchair, he was determined to continue his ambitious political career and became the first and only disabled American to be elected president. During his presidency, Roosevelt was a tireless advocate for the disabled and a strong promoter of the effort to identify a cure for polio.

Unfortunately for many polio patients, the virus destroyed the nerves supplying the respiratory muscles—the diaphragm and the intercostals, the muscles between the ribs. These patients would often suffocate because they were unable to contract their diaphragm and external intercostals to draw air into their lungs. Some polio sufferers were afraid to fall asleep at night for fear they would stop breathing and never wake up.

To help polio patients breathe, a Harvard University engineer named Philip Drinker designed the "iron lung" in the late 1920s (Figure 6.6). His machine consisted of an airtight chamber in which the entire body except for the head was enclosed. The iron lung made use of electrically driven bellows that created negative pressure in the chamber, forcing the diaphragm to contract. Contraction of the diaphragm lowered the air pressure within the lung below that of the atmosphere, and air flowed into the lungs. The pressure in the chamber was then allowed to increase, causing the diaphragm and rib cage to return to their resting state. The volume of the lung decreased, lung pressure increased above atmospheric pressure, and air was forced out of the lungs.

A less bulky version of the iron lung was developed by the manufacturer of the device, John Emerson (grandson of Ralph Waldo Emerson), and widely used until the late 1950s.

Jonas Salk developed the first polio vaccine based on injections of weakened, but live, polio virus. Beginning in 1955, students in the United States lined up at their schools to receive their polio shots. A safer polio vaccine was made available soon after due to the efforts of Albert Bruce Sabin. The Sabin polio vaccine was also live, but the disease-causing portions of the virus were disabled, and the vaccine could also be taken orally. Beginning in the early 1960s, students were lining up in schools to receive their bright pink sugar cube that contained the Sabin vaccine.

The number of polio cases dropped from 2,252 in 1960 to 61 in 1965. Not a single case of polio has been reported in the United States since 1979. However, in undeveloped countries, the incidence of polio is much higher, and the disease has yet to be eliminated from the world.

There are only a few remaining polio patients who still make use of the iron lung to help them breathe. Some of these patients have spent 40 to 50 years of their life lying enclosed in this machine, too afraid to switch to the portable respirators available today (similar to the one that actor Christopher Reeve uses). Modern-day respirators make use of positive pressure to drive air into the lungs rather than negative pressure applied to the chest. The design principle behind both of these "breathing machines" is the same; both create differences in air pressure to force air in and out of the lungs.

Figure 6.6 Shown here is a photograph of a polio patient making use of an iron lung, or negative pressure chamber, to assist with breathing. Such machines have since been replaced with positive pressure respirators that force air into the lung.

(Continued from page 59)

DEAD AIR

Air remains in the lungs after a person has exhaled with maximal force and even more air remains after a quiet exhalation. The air that remains in the lungs affects the rate of oxygen diffusion in the blood. Because in mammals, air flows in and out of the lungs using the same pathway, incoming fresh air with its higher oxygen content mixes with the remaining air that has a lower oxygen content.

At sea level, atmospheric PO_2 is 160 mm Hg. However, the oxygen concentration of air at the surface of the alveoli is only 100 mm Hg. Incoming atmospheric air (160 mm Hg) mixes with the air remaining in the lungs, referred to as **dead air**, which has a PO_2 of 40 mm Hg. According to Fick's law, this resulting decrease in the partial pressure gradient for oxygen (P_2-P_1) diminishes the rate of oxygen diffusion into the blood.

In contrast to the mammalian lung, birds have evolved a unidirectional flow-through lung that avoids the problem of diluting the incoming fresh air with so-called dead air. This fact may come as no surprise to those mountain climbers who have observed snow geese flying vigorously overhead while they stood gasping for air on the summit of a high mountain.

CONNECTIONS

To take a breath, or inspire, the volume of the human lung increases, thus creating a region of lower pressure. Air rushes into the lungs until lung pressure is equal to atmospheric pressure. To move air out of the lungs, a process known as expiration, the volume of the lung is decreased. As a result, lung pressure increases above atmospheric levels and air moves out. The changes in lung volume are accomplished by the actions of the respiratory muscles, the diaphram and the intercostals. Inspiration is an active process, while expiration is typically passive.

A spirometer is used to measure respiratory volumes and is one of the important tools used to assess a patient's respiratory health. Air remains in the lungs following even the most forceful expiration. This air, known as dead air, has a low O_2 content and dilutes the fresh air entering the lungs with the next breath. As a result, the PO_2 of air in the lungs is much lower than that of the atmosphere.

7

Preventing Collapse of the Lungs

There is always a considerable amount of air remaining in the lungs, called the residual volume, even after a maximally forceful expiration. The residual volume is important for keeping our lungs partially inflated. In this chapter, you will learn what prevents air from leaving the lungs and why it is important to keep the lungs partially inflated.

PNEUMOTHORAX AND LUNG PRESSURE

We can get an idea of the consequences of lung collapse by looking at a condition known as **pneumothorax**, a collection of air or gas in the space that surrounds the lungs (the pleural space). When an individual sustains a penetrating injury to the thoracic cavity (such as a gunshot or stab wound), he or she runs the risk of having one or both of the lungs collapse, as air leaks from the lungs through the chest wall and enters the pleural space. Under such circumstances, the ability to breathe is severely compromised.

The lungs are surrounded by two pleural membranes. The existence of the pleural membranes, the parietal and visceral pleura, and the fluid-filled cavity known as the pleural cavity, were described in Chapter 4. The pleural membranes for the right and left lung are separate from each other. The pressure within the pleural cavity is about 4 mm Hg below that of the atmosphere (i.e., at sea level about 756 mm Hg).

Figure 7.1 The surface tension of water at an air-water interface is strong enough to support the weight of a water strider, shown here. This force arises from the physical arrangement of the water molecules at the surface.

Recall that the visceral membrane adheres to the outer surface of the lungs. Between breaths, the negative pressure within the pleural cavity (i.e., negative relative to lung and atmospheric pressure) prevents the elastic lung tissue from completely collapsing in upon itself. If an object, such as a bullet or knife, penetrates the pleural cavity, air will be sucked into the cavity and the pressure within the cavity will equalize with atmospheric pressure. In the absence of the negative pressure within the pleural cavity, the lung will partially or fully collapse. As a consequence, gas exchange will be severely compromised in affected regions of the lung.

ALVEOLAR SURFACE TENSION

Another factor that promotes lung collapse is **alveolar surface tension**. The alveolar surface is moist and in contact with the air in the lungs. Wherever water and air form an interface, the water molecules are physically arranged in a particular pattern that creates tension at its surface. Possessing surface tension when in contact with air is one of the important physical properties of water. In fact, this property is of sufficient strength to support the weight of water striders on the surface of a pond or stream (Figure 7.1).

Water molecules are attracted to other water molecules. Because of the spherical shape and small diameters of the alveoli, tension is exerted by neighboring water molecules coating the inner surface of this sphere, drawing in the alveolar walls and promoting collapse (Figure 7.2). Because alveolar surface tension increases as the diameter of the alveoli decreases, this pull gets greater as the lungs deflate.

Surfactants

The type II alveolar cells secrete compounds that greatly reduce the surface tension within the alveoli as their diameters decrease during expiration. **Surfactants** are lipoproteins, or protein molecules with a lipid component. By coating the alveolar surfaces and physically disrupting the arrangement of the water molecules present there, they reduce surface tension and prevent collapse of the alveoli. Because these molecules coat the inner surface of the lungs, when the lung volume decreases, the surfactant molecules bunch up and become even more effective at reducing the surface tension of water. In this way, the effectiveness of surfactant coincides with the point in the breathing cycle at which alveolar surface tension is greatest.

INFANT RESPIRATORY DISTRESS SYNDROME

The human fetus obtains its oxygen from the mother's blood supply and does not use its lungs for respiration while in the uterus. The human fetus starts manufacturing pulmonary surfactants after seven months *in utero*. Infants that are born more than two months premature often suffer from **infant respiratory distress syndrome,** or **IRDS** (Figure 7.3). The absence of surfactants causes the premature infant's alveoli to collapse every time it exhales. To overcome the high alveolar surface tension created under this situation, an enormous amount of

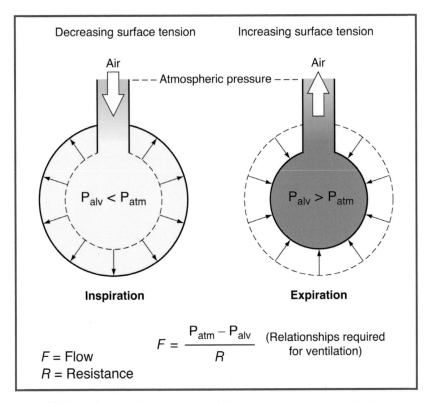

Figure 7.2 As the diameter of the alveolus decreases with the expiration process, the force due to the surface tension of water increases, promoting alveolar collapse.

energy is required to reinflate the lungs with every breathing cycle. As a consequence, babies with IRDS become rapidly fatigued.

This lung disorder affects 10% of all premature infants and is only rarely seen in full-term babies. The symptoms include a rapid breathing rate, nasal flaring, grunting sounds while breathing, and bluish coloration of the skin. Low O_2 and high CO_2 levels as detected by blood gas analysis will confirm the presence of the disorder.

IRDS once claimed the lives of as many as 25,000 to 30,000 infants, but the number of fatalities has been greatly reduced. Treatment for babies with IRDS may include the use of

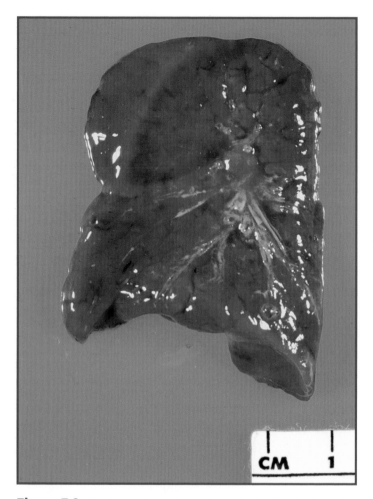

Figure 7.3 The hemorrhaged lung of an infant with infant respiratory distress syndrome, or IRDS, is shown here. This disease, which affects 10% of all premature babies, is caused by a lack of pulmonary surfactant. Without surfactants, the alveoli of the lung collapse and the infant cannot breathe properly.

oxygen supplementation and positive pressure ventilation to keep the lungs inflated between breaths. The administration of surfactants to the infant's lung surface is also a common procedure. Researchers are now attempting to develop artificial surfactants for that purpose. The treatments are designed to keep the infant alive until its lungs start to produce surfactants. Despite treatment, IRDS remains the number one cause of death in premature infants. IRDS is one of the primary reasons that obstetricians try hard to prevent expectant mothers from experiencing a premature delivery.

CONNECTIONS

The elastic nature of lung tissue and the forces exerted by surface tension within each small alveoli combine to promote the collapse of the lungs. The negative pressure within each pleural cavity serves to keep the lungs from fully deflating with each expiration. Type II alveolar cells make surfactants that disrupt the surface tension of the water molecules lining the lung tissue. The important function of the surfactants is underscored by the condition IRDS. In this disease of premature infants, the lack of pulmonary surfactant makes breathing an energetically draining process that can lead to death if left untreated.

8

How the Respiratory System Adjusts to Meet Changing Oxygen Demands

The respiratory system is able to respond to changes in a person's activity level. Whether the person is sleeping, walking, or running, the breathing rate changes to meet the demands of the particular activity. Increased levels of activity are accompanied by an increased need for ATP and, therefore, an increased need for oxygen.

In this chapter you will learn how respiratory functions are controlled by the body and you will explore how the human body senses changes in the need for oxygen and relays that information to the respiratory system so that the appropriate adjustments can be made.

NEURAL CONTROL OF BREATHING

The **medulla oblongata** of the brainstem contains neurons (nerve cells) that control breathing movements. Some of the neurons are called **inspiratory neurons** because they fire during inspiration. Other neurons have been identified as **expiratory neurons** because they fire only during expiration. Both the inspiratory and expiratory

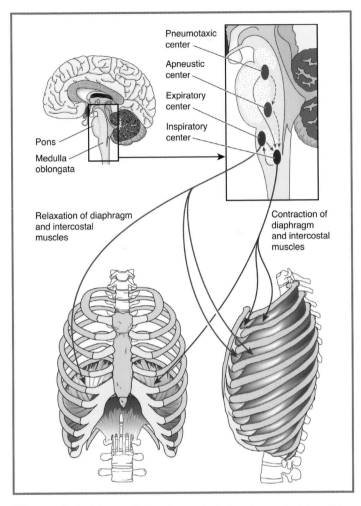

Figure 8.1 The medulla oblongata helps to control breathing and respiration. The respiratory control centers of the medulla oblongata and pons regions of the brainstem and the respiratory muscles they stimulate are illustrated here. A signal is sent from the expiratory and inspiratory centers on the medulla that tells the diaphragm and intercostal muscles to contract or relax.

neurons project down into the spinal cord and connect with other neurons that carry signals to the respiratory muscles (the diaphragm and the intercostal muscles) (Figure 8.1).

Most of the inspiratory neurons of the medulla are clustered together in what is known as the **inspiratory center**. When these neurons fire, they stimulate the diaphragm and external inter-costals to contract, so the person inhales. If the frequency of the firing rate of the inspiratory center neurons increases, then the person will take a deeper breath, increasing the tidal volume. If they fire for a longer period of time, then you will take a slower (longer) breath. When they stop firing, the diaphragm and external intercostals will relax, and the person will exhale (passively).

Most of the expiratory neurons of the medulla are clustered together in what is known as the **expiratory center**. Under typical conditions, the neurons of the expiratory center are inactive. They fire only when it is necessary to exhale more deeply, as with a forced expiration. Their firing inhibits the inspiratory center neurons from firing. When there is a need for a deep inspiration, the inspiratory center neurons can also prevent the expiratory center from firing.

Together, these two respiratory centers of the medulla are responsible for our rhythmic breathing patterns. Scientists are still working to identify how the breathing rhythm is established.

Another group of neurons in a different region of the brain-stem, the **pons**, is responsible for setting the rhythm of the firing of the inspiratory center (refer again to Figure 8.1). These neurons can be found in what is called the **pneumotaxic area** of the pons, and they transmit their impulses to the inspiratory center. When the signals from the pneumotaxic area are weak, the rate of breathing slows. When the signals from the pneumotaxic area increase in intensity, the rate of breathing increases. In other words, the pneumotaxic area of the pons controls our breathing rate through its control of respiratory centers in the brainstem.

The apneustic center is located between the pneumotaxic and expiratory centers. Its role in respiration is not well understood.

CHEMORECEPTORS AND BREATHING PATTERNS

The body senses changes in oxygen status and relays that informa-tion to these control centers through the use of chemoreceptors.

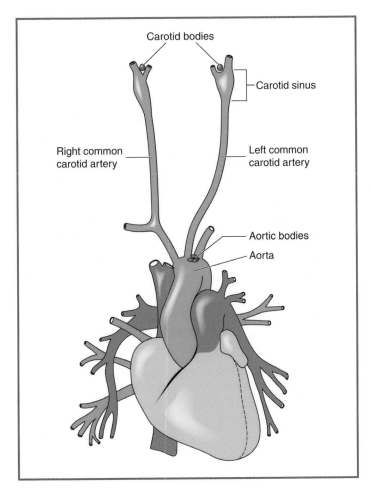

Carotid bodies

Carotid sinus

Right common
carotid artery

Left common
carotid artery

Aortic bodies

Aorta

Figure 8.2 The peripheral chemoreceptors (or bodies) are located in the aortic arch and carotid arteries. The central chemoreceptors are located in the medulla oblongata of the brainstem (not shown). The chemoreceptors monitor the amount of oxygen that the respiratory system is providing to the blood and help adjust this amount if necessary.

Chemoreceptors are sensory neurons that are sensitive to changes in blood gases and other chemicals that indicate whether the respiratory function is matching the need for oxygen. There are two locations for these specialized cells in the body (Figure 8.2).

(Continued on page 78)

WHY DO WE YAWN?

In addition to breathing movements, our respiratory system moves air in response to a variety of stimuli. These movements are collectively called nonrespiratory movements. Examples of these include hiccupping, coughing, sneezing, and yawning.

Humans yawn when they are becoming tired. According to studies, however, humans also yawn when they are waking, leading researchers to suggest that yawning is an activity that accompanies any change in our state of alertness.

The yawning process follows a typical pattern of a single deep inspiration. The mouth is open and the jaw and chest muscles get stretched to accommodate this action. Scientists have identified the yawning center of the brain in the **paraventricular nucleus** of the hypothalamus, situated near the base of the brain. For some unknown reason, certain individuals, such as those with multiple sclerosis and brain damage, suffer from bouts of excessive yawning. Studying these patients will likely help in learning more about the neural control of yawning.

Researchers hypothesize that the trigger for initiating a yawn is the presence of low oxygen levels in the lung. Shallow breaths do not work as efficiently as deeper breaths at exchanging fresh air for dead air during respiration. Taking a deep breath may help to ventilate the entire lung and open and stretch alveoli that were not being used before the yawn. Scientists have also hypothesized that expansion of the lung may aid in the spread of surfactants across the entire surface, maintaining a low surface tension and reducing the energy required for inspiration.

However, these physiological explanations do little to address other observations about yawning. If yawning is triggered solely by low O_2 levels in the lung, then why is yawning so contagious? It appears that even discussing or thinking about yawning is suggestive and promotes yawning. Yawning in other animal groups appears to represent some form of communication, possibly for the purpose of synchronizing behavior. In addition, scientists have yet to uncover any means by which lungs can directly sense their O_2 levels. If low O_2 levels in the lung are the stimulus, then there must be some mechanism in the lung for sensing such changes.

Whatever the stimulus for yawning, it appears that there is some feedback mechanism in play. If a person stifles a yawn by not opening the mouth or not allowing the jaw and chest muscles to stretch, then the stimulus for yawning will continue until a full yawn is completed.

BOX 8.1 Why do people yawn, and why is yawning so contagious? There is much to learn about this puzzling nonrespiratory movement.

(Continued from page 75)

Peripheral chemoreceptors are located in the carotid arteries and the aortic arch. **Central chemoreceptors** are located in the respiratory centers of the brainstem.

Peripheral chemoreceptors are sensitive to the oxygen levels of the blood. When blood PO_2 levels drop, the peripheral chemoreceptors fire, stimulating the inspiratory center neurons of the medulla to increase both the breathing rate and the tidal volume. However, oxygen levels have to be low for this response to be triggered.

The central chemoreceptors are insensitive to blood PO_2 levels altogether and are far more sensitive to changes in PCO_2 and pH levels of the blood than are the peripheral chemoreceptors. As a waste product of cellular respiration, CO_2 must be eliminated from the blood by the respiratory system during expiration. A buildup of CO_2 within the blood can indicate that the breathing rate and rate of expiration is too slow. When CO_2 levels in the blood begin to increase, the central chemoreceptors become activated, stimulating the respiratory centers of the brainstem to increase the breathing rate. This leads to the elimination of excess CO_2 in the blood.

The **pH** is a measure of hydrogen ion (H^+) concentration. An increase in pH indicates a decrease in $[H^+]$ and a decrease in acidity. Conversely, a decrease in pH indicates an increase in $[H^+]$ and an increase in acidity. When CO_2 is dissolved in water, the primary component of blood, it reacts with water to form carbonic acid (Figure 8.3). Carbonic acid dissociates into a bicarbonate ion and a hydrogen ion. For this reason, as CO_2 levels build up in the blood, there is a corresponding increase in $[H^+]$ and a decrease in pH. If the body does not eliminate CO_2 efficiently, the blood will become too acidic and important functions may be impaired.

When PCO_2 levels rise and/or pH levels drop, the central chemoreceptors signal the respiratory centers to increase the breathing rate to increase the rate of CO_2 elimination. Once the

$$CO_2 + H_2O \longrightarrow H_2CO_3 \longrightarrow HCO_3^- + H^+$$
(Carbon Dioxide + Water ⟹ Carbonic Acid ⟹ Bicarbonate + Hydrogen Ions)

Increase in CO_2 ⟶ increase in $[H^+]$ ⟶ decrease in pH

Decrease in CO_2 ⟶ decrease in $[H^+]$ ⟶ increase in pH

Figure 8.3 This figure shows the chemical reaction illustrating the relationship between CO_2, $[H^+]$, and pH of the blood. As CO_2 levels in the blood increase, the amount of hydrogen ions increases, causing a decrease in the pH of the blood.

levels of CO_2 and $[H^+]$ in the blood return to normal, the central chemoreceptors stop firing.

Sometimes individuals who are emotionally upset unintentionally hyperventilate, or breathe rapidly. With hyperventilation, too much CO_2 can be exhaled and the pH of the blood begins to rise. The rise in blood pH can partially close off arteries bringing blood to the brain, thereby reducing flow to the brain and triggering a fainting response. Individuals who are unintentionally hyperventilating are often given a paper bag in which to breathe. CO_2 levels build up in the paper bag as the individual rebreathes the air, eventually helping the blood CO_2 levels to return to normal.

HOW THE RESPIRATORY SYSTEM ADJUSTS TO CHANGES: EXERCISE

As discussed in Chapter 3, any human activity that results in an increased demand for ATP also increases the body's requirement for oxygen. The respiratory system will make the necessary adjustments to attempt to meet that change in demand.

During exercise, the skeletal muscles require more ATP and oxygen to contract. Not all of the mechanisms designed to increase the oxygen supply to these tissues involve the respiratory system. For example, blood flow will be directed away from tissues like the digestive tract and redirected to the active muscles. In this way, the amount of oxygen-rich blood received by the skeletal muscles is enhanced to meet their increased need for oxygen.

The respiratory system, however, is responsible for ensuring that the blood supply flowing to the active muscles is completely saturated with oxygen. The inspiratory center of the brainstem stimulates the respiratory muscles to increase the tidal volume (deeper breaths) and, to a lesser degree, increase the breathing rate. In the case of strenuous physical exercise, the expiratory center will also be stimulated so that forced expirations occur, reducing the amount of dead air residing in the lungs after expiration. Because dead air is of lower oxygen content, this response effectively reduces the degree to which incoming fresh air is diluted. It has been estimated that with vigorous exercise, the amount of air ventilating the lungs per unit time can increase by more than 10-fold over resting values in humans.

It is not clear what initiates the respiratory system's responses to exercise. It would be reasonable to predict that increased activity translates to increased rates of cellular respiration and, therefore, to reduced PO_2 and increased CO_2 levels in the blood. The peripheral and central chemoreceptors would detect these changes and activate the appropriate respiratory centers in the brainstem. However, respiratory physiologists have not found significant changes in blood CO_2 and O_2 levels to be correlated with exercise.

It has also been noted that some of the physiological responses to exercise occur before the start of exercise. Humans have some conscious control over their breathing rate and the mere anticipation of exercise can increase our level of respiratory function. It would also appear that another region of the brain, the cerebral cortex, relays signals to the respiratory centers of the brainstem in response to the changes in joint activity and muscle contraction that accompany exercise. In short, although additional research will be required before there are definitive answers to this question, the cerebral cortex, in response to changes in muscle and joint activity and to mental input, represents a key trigger for enhanced respiratory function during exercise.

HOW THE RESPIRATORY SYSTEM
ADJUSTS TO CHANGES: HIGH ALTITUDE

The low O_2 levels of high-altitude environments present challenges to those humans who choose to inhabit them either temporarily or permanently. As with exercise, changes in respiratory function represent only one of many physiological responses to high-altitude exposure. These responses can be categorized into short-term and long-term responses.

Short-term responses occur immediately upon exposure to high altitude. These consist of a variety of rather uncoordinated physiological reactions that may not always be in the best interest of the individual's health. Typically, after one to three days of exposure, however, long-term physiological responses begin and the individual starts to **acclimate**, or adapt, to high altitude. There is a great deal of variation in the ability of individuals to make these adaptations, however. As Jon Krakauer describes in his book *Into Thin Air*, despite spending days at high altitude to allow time for acclimation, many on the Everest expedition never became acclimated and had to return to lower elevations or risk death.

The reduced PO_2 levels of the high-altitude environment immediately reduce oxygen levels in the blood, a condition called **hypoxia**. Hypoxia triggers the peripheral chemoreceptors to stimulate the inspiratory center of the brainstem. As a result, both the breathing rate and tidal volume increase. The blood PCO_2 levels drop as more carbon dioxide is exhaled. The reduction in blood PCO_2 can lead to alkalosis, a condition where the blood pH is higher than normal.

The low blood PO_2 levels that occur when a person moves abruptly to high altitude can cause additional symptoms as well. These symptoms, collectively known as **acute mountain sickness**, or **AMS**, include fatigue, lack of appetite, distorted vision, headache, confusion, nausea, and dizziness. About 75% of all individuals will exhibit mild to moderate symptoms of AMS at altitudes of 10,000 feet and above (many western U.S. ski resorts approach this elevation). For most of the population, the symptoms associated with AMS disappear or lessen after two to three days because of the onset of more long-term responses to life at high altitude. The kidneys make adjustments such that blood pH returns to normal. The oxygen-carrying capacity of the blood is enhanced, helping to compensate for the low atmospheric PO_2 levels. Breathing rate and tidal volume remain elevated above low-altitude values. Despite several days of acclimation, however, certain tasks, such as strenuous physical exertion and memorization, will remain difficult.

In severe cases, high-altitude exposure becomes life-threatening. For example, the extra work required of the respiratory and circulatory systems can lead to heart failure. A more common severe response is **pulmonary edema**, the accumulation of fluid in the lungs. When associated with high-altitude exposure, it is called **high-altitude pulmonary edema**, or **HAPE**. For reasons not well understood, pressure forces fluid to leak from the blood (in the pulmonary capillaries) into the interstitial and alveolar spaces of the lung tissue. This action will increase the diffusion distance for oxygen and, according to Fick's law, PO_2 levels will decrease even further into a dangerous spiral downward.

Healthy young males in their twenties are the most susceptible to HAPE. Typically, it occurs with strenuous physical activity incurred immediately after arrival at high altitude. Milder cases can be treated at altitude with oxygen therapy and rest. Many western U.S. ski resorts are well-equipped to help relieve symptoms of mild to moderate cases of HAPE and also are ready to transport individuals with severe cases to medical facilities at lower altitudes.

CONNECTIONS

The respiratory system is able to adjust to changes in the body's activity level. Respiratory centers located in the medulla oblongata region of the brainstem regulate the activity of the respiratory muscles through nervous input. The activity of the respiratory centers can be altered by changes in blood chemistry as detected by peripheral and central chemoreceptors. A drop in PO_2 or a rise in CO_2 or H^+ levels in the blood will trigger an increase in respiration via an increase in tidal volume and increased breathing rate.

Respiratory responses to exercise appear to be initiated by the cerebral cortex in response to increased joint and muscle activity as well as to psychic input. The low PO_2 levels associated with high-altitude environments pose a challenge to both respiratory and circulatory functions in humans. Although most individuals eventually acclimate to high-altitude exposure within two to three days, many suffer from symptoms of acute mountain sickness upon initial exposure. HAPE, or high-altitude pulmonary edema, represents a life-threatening physiological response to high altitude and requires immediate treatment.

9

Respiratory Disease

At this point, you should have an understanding of the importance of respiration and the structure and function of the human lung in health. There are diseases, however, that can interfere with normal lung function. In this chapter, you will learn about some of the more common human respiratory ailments, such as asthma and emphysema.

Asthma and emphysema are included in a larger group of respiratory disorders known as chronic obstructive pulmonary disease, or COPD. As outlined in Chapter 4, air must move through a series of airways before reaching the site of exchange in the lungs. We'll learn how asthma can severely interfere with that flow. Emphysema interferes with breathing through its effects on the elasticity of the lung tissue itself. We will also examine an infectious disease of the lung, tuberculosis, and learn why it is becoming more common.

In this chapter, we will also address the devastating health and societal impact of a common addiction, cigarette smoking.

CHRONIC OBSTRUCTIVE PULMONARY DISEASE: ASTHMA

Once a rare disorder, **asthma** has grown to epidemic proportions. Asthma is a condition in which the airway passages constrict, causing intense wheezing and coughing. In the United States alone, more

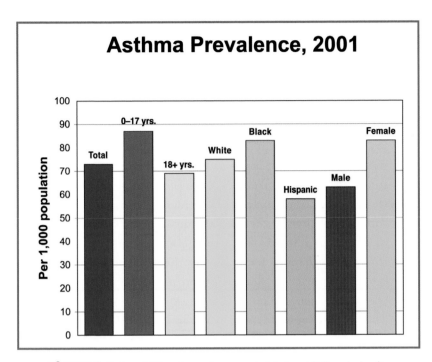

Figure 9.1 In addition to an increased risk for childhood obesity and diabetes, children who spend a great deal of time indoors are more likely to suffer from asthma. This graph, based upon data from the Centers for Disease Control and Prevention (CDC), displays the prevalence of asthma among several groups (age, race, and gender) for 2001.

than 15 million individuals suffer from asthma, resulting in 5,000 deaths per year (180,000 deaths annually worldwide). Asthma occurs with much greater frequency in Western countries.

Although there does appear to be a genetic component to this disease, the incidence of asthma is primarily associated with lifestyle and environment. Researchers argue that asthma is more common in children today (Figure 9.1) because they spend far more time indoors rather than outdoors and, as a result, have greater exposure to household allergens including pet dander and the feces of dust mites and cockroaches. Asthma can also be induced by exercise, infection, emotional stress, temperature, or exposure to pollen, household chemicals, dyes, cosmetics, and air pollutants.

Airborne allergens such as pollen or chemical irritants enter the upper airways of the respiratory system when a person inhales. Often these particles are trapped in the mucus layer lining these regions, where the cilia move the offending particles up and out of the lungs. In some cases, however, these particles make it past the upper airway regions, reaching the smaller airways, like the bronchioles, that do not have a ciliated lining. Once these particles enter the bronchioles, they continuously irritate the smooth muscle cells, initiating an inflammatory response and swelling. Because the bronchioles have no mechanism for removing the offending irritants, bronchoconstriction, or a reduction in the diameter of the bronchioles, may also result.

With the bronchioles narrowed, an individual has a much harder time ventilating his or her lungs. It is especially hard to exhale air. When the person with narrowed bronchioles exhales, the person generates the wheezing sounds characteristic of asthma. Asthma patients must have medicine handy to keep their airways open, thus preventing an asthma attack (Figure 9.2). These medicines fall into two classes of drugs: bronchodilators and anti-inflammatory medications. Bronchodilators relax the constricted bronchiolar smooth muscle, increasing the diameter of the bronchioles. The anti-inflammatory drugs, like corticosteroids, inhibit the inflammatory response triggered by the presence of allergens in the airways, preventing tissue swelling and reducing secretions. A severe asthma attack will require an emergency room visit to establish an open airway and prevent suffocation.

CHRONIC OBSTRUCTIVE PULMONARY DISEASE: EMPHYSEMA

Emphysema is another chronic obstructive pulmonary disease that occurs in nearly 3 million Americans. In the disease emphysema, the alveolar sacs have lost their elasticity and remain in an overinflated state. As a result, it is very difficult to

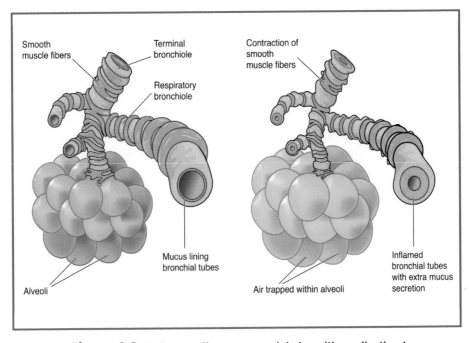

Smooth
muscle fibers

Terminal
bronchiole

Respiratory
bronchiole

Contraction of
smooth
muscle fibers

Mucus lining
bronchial tubes

Air trapped within alveoli

Inflamed
bronchial tubes
with extra mucus
secretion

Alveoli

Figure 9.2 Asthma sufferers use an inhaler with medication to help open their constricted airways. A normal airway is shown on the left; a constricted airway is illustrated on the right.

exchange the air in the alveoli efficiently and thus the partial pressure gradient for oxygen uptake is reduced. Patients initially experience bouts of breathlessness and coughing, and their ability to be active becomes very limited. Eventually, the alveoli become permanently damaged, and whole regions of the lung are unable to be engaged in gas exchange with the blood.

The most common cause of emphysema is cigarette smoking (80–90% of emphysema cases). Cigarette smoke paralyzes respiratory cilia, rendering them unable to remove particulate matter (also present in cigarette smoke) from the lungs. The presence of particulates in cigarette smoke causes pulmonary immune cells to release defense molecules, including enzymes that damage the delicate alveolar tissue. For some emphysema patients, the lack of a protein known as alpha 1-antitrypsin (AAT) is responsible for a hereditary form of the disease. Although there is no cure for emphysema, behavioral changes and other treatments can reduce the rate of lung degeneration and help to relieve the symptoms.

Currently, 25% of the adult population smokes. Smokers are more likely to be young males (aged 18–24), although smoking is fairly prevalent across all age groups. With respect to race and ethnicity, Native American populations have the highest smoking rate, and Hispanic and Asian populations exhibit the lowest rates. With respect to educational background, there is a substantial decline in the incidence of smoking with increasing years of education. College graduates exhibit lower rates when compared to those with a high school education or less.

Smoking has a significant detrimental impact on our society's collective health. Smoking-related diseases *kill* almost 450,000 Americans annually. The amount of money lost each year to the treatment of smoking-related disorders combined with the loss in employee productivity is estimated to be a staggering $150 billion.

Smoking affects health in many ways. At least 43 different cancer-causing chemicals have been detected in cigarette smoke. About 87% of all lung cancer cases are due to smoking. Smoking is responsible for the majority of cases of emphysema and chronic bronchitis, and is a major contributor to increased incidence of heart disease and stroke. Smoking also increases an individual's risk for other cancers, ulcers, and reduced fertility. Smoking during pregnancy negatively impacts the infant's birth weight and lung function.

Exposure to secondhand smoke also poses a hazard. Children whose parents smoke have higher incidences of asthma, colds, and ear infections. Secondhand smoke exposure accounts for 3,000 of the 160,000 deaths attributed to lung cancer annually.

When an individual breathes in cigarette smoke, he or she

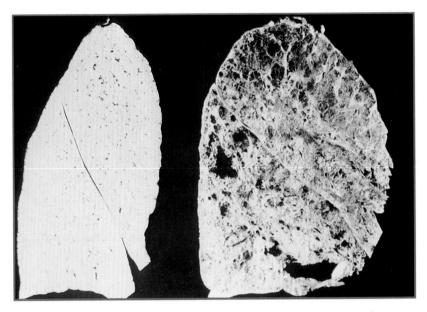

Figure 9.2 In the United States, 25% of the adult population smoke cigarettes and, as a result, are at increased risk for emphysema, chronic bronchitis, lung cancer, heart disease, and stroke. The lung on the left is that of a nonsmoker; the lung on the right is from a person who smoked.

does more than expose the sensitive lung tissue to carcinogens that promote lung cancer. As indicated previously, the smoke paralyzes the cilia of the epithelial lining of the airways. Debris and mucus cannot be removed from the lung, and there is an increased risk of infection. Without cilia, smokers must cough to bring up mucus, and this chronic coughing often leads to chronic bronchitis. This progressive deterioration of the smaller airways will likely continue until emphysema results from the loss of alveolar elasticity due to chronic coughing and increased infections (Figure 9.2).

In addition to these debilitating effects, as discussed previously, exposure to carcinogens may lead to lung cancer. There are two major types of cancer: small cell lung cancer and non-small cell lung cancer. Non-small cell lung cancer is far more common, accounting for 80% of cases, and is the less malignant form (slower to spread to other body regions). The more cigarettes an individual smokes per day and the longer he or she smokes are both important determinants of the risk for getting lung cancer.

Unfortunately, it is difficult to detect lung cancer in its early stages because there are no symptoms. Lung cancer is typically detected in later stages by X-ray or computerized tomography (CT) imaging following complaints such as wheezing, coughing, hoarseness, weight and appetite loss, fever, chest pain, chronic bronchitis, pneumonia, or shortness of breath. Lung cancer treatment usually involves surgical removal of diseased portions of lung, chemotherapy, and/or radiation therapy. Lung cancer treatments are not effective in the long term. Only 13% of treated lung cancer patients live beyond 5 years after diagnosis.

If you currently smoke, you can significantly reduce your risk for acquiring all of these smoke-related diseases by stopping now. The respiratory system is, for the most part, able to repair the damage caused by smoking and return to a relatively healthier state. Unfortunately, it is hard to quit smoking, since the nicotine in cigarette smoke is so addictive. When inhaled, nicotine reaches the brain faster than if it were delivered intravenously. The use of nicotine replacement strategies, in which nicotine patches, inhalers, gum, and nasal sprays help to alleviate nicotine cravings, allows the smoker time to stop the other habits he or she associates with lighting up.

INFECTIOUS LUNG DISEASE: TUBERCULOSIS

The lung infection tuberculosis (TB) is caused by the bacterium *Mycobacterium tuberculosis*. Although this disease was common in the early 20th century, it now only inflicts about 18,000 Americans annually. When a person is infected with the TB bacterium, the lung tissue responds by forming knots of tough fibrous connective tissue around the sites of infection (Figure 9.3). The resulting structures, called

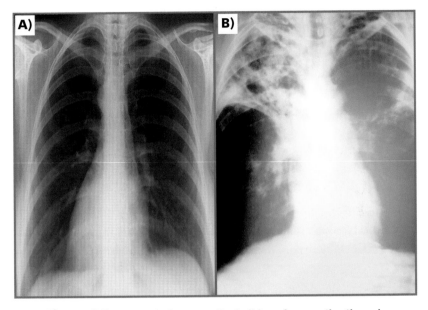

Figure 9.3 Tuberculosis causes the buildup of connective tissue in the lungs, call tubercles. Although the tubercles help to prevent further spread of the tuberculosis bacterium, they also make gas exchange difficult and impair breathing. Figure (A) shows a normal chest X-ray; Figure (B) shows an X-ray image of the lungs of a TB patient.

tubercles, help prevent the spread of the bacteria. The number of these tubercles may increase to a point where gas exchange is severely compromised because of the increased thickness of the respiratory barrier. Alternatively, if the bacterium overwhelms the ability of the lung to thwart widespread infection, the resulting tissue damage will likewise impair respiratory function.

Tuberculosis is highly contagious and can be spread by airborne droplets produced by coughing and sneezing. An infected individual may not experience symptoms until years after being infected or the individual may become immediately ill, if he or she is already in poor health. According to the American Lung Association, symptoms include a persistent cough, chronic fatigue, weight loss, appetite loss, blood in mucus that has been coughed up, and night sweats. Skin tests and chest X-rays are used to confirm a diagnosis of TB.

By 1992, the incidence of TB had risen by more than 20% after decreasing steadily since the 1940s. Much of this increase accompanied the epidemic of acquired immune deficiency syndrome, or AIDS, because the compromised immune systems of AIDS patients increased their susceptibility to infection. Since 1992, disease prevention strategies have reversed the trend in TB cases.

TB remains an international problem. In 1999, the World Health Organization reported that nearly one-third of the world's population was infected. Indeed, many of the TB cases in the United States involve people of foreign origin.

The standard treatment for TB infection is designed to prevent the onset of the full-blown disease. This is typically accomplished through a nine-month daily regimen of the drug isoniazid. An individual suffering from the full-blown disease will receive a particular combination of drugs until lung function returns to normal and the person is no longer capable of infecting others. In both cases, patients need to be monitored regularly to ensure they continue their drug therapy. Otherwise, they risk getting sick again and/or promoting the development of a drug-resistant strain of TB that is more difficult to treat. The incidence of drug-resistant strains of TB is rising rapidly worldwide much to the alarm of healthcare professionals. In the United States, New York City and California report the highest incidence of the deadly, multi-drug-resistant forms of TB.

CONNECTIONS

Respiration is essential for life. Without it, our cells are deprived of the oxygen required for cellular respiration, the process that converts food energy to ATP, the only form of energy our active cells can use. There are many diseases and conditions that can interfere with respiration. Some, like asthma, may be caused by a combination of genetics and environmental influences. Others, like tuberculosis, are contagious and are therefore more prevalent where sanitation is poor and health care is unavailable. Cigarette smoking damages the lungs and increases the risk for a variety of respiratory diseases, including lung cancer.

Glossary

Acclimate To adapt to certain conditions, such as high altitude.

Acute Mountain Sickness (AMS) Condition that can occur when the body is at high altitude. Symptoms range depending on the severity of the sickness, but can include headache, dizziness, fatigue, shortness of breath, loss of appetite, vomiting, and nausea.

Adenosine Triphosphate Also known as ATP, the molecule that stores and releases energy for use in the cells.

Alveolar Ducts One of the gradually narrowing airway passages in the lungs through which air passes, branching from the respiratory bronchioles and into alveoli.

Alveolar Surface Tension Tension created within the alveoli because of the gas-liquid interface in which the liquid molecules are drawn more closely together and resist the force to increase the surface area within the alveoli.

Alveoli Small hollow sacs in the lungs where the bulk of gas exchange with the blood occurs. Singular is alveolus.

Asthma Condition in which the airway passages constrict the movement of air, causing the person to wheeze and cough. An asthma attack can be brought on by many factors, including allergies, exercise, or stress.

Barometric Pressure Also known as total atmospheric pressure, the force per unit area exerted against a surface by the weight of the air molecules above that surface.

Basal Metabolic Rate Also known as BMR, the amount of energy the body needs to perform activities, such as breathing, per hour.

Boyle's Law Also known as the ideal gas law, law stating that when the temperature is constant, the pressure of a gas changes according to its volume. Thus, when the volume of a container holding gas increases, the pressure of the gas within the container decreases.

Bronchi Two large branches from the trachea that lead to the lungs, dividing into gradually narrower passages.

Bronchioles Air passages, less than 1 mm in diameter, that connect the bronchi to the alveoli.

Bulk Flow Movement of fluids or gases from region of higher pressure to one of lower pressure.

Cellular Respiration Also known as cellular metabolism, a group of reactions during which food fuels, particularly glucose, are broken down within cells and some of the energy released is captured to form adenosine triphosphate (ATP).

Central Chemoreceptors Sensory receptors that are located in the respiratory centers of the brainstem.

Chemoreceptors Sensory receptors that detect changes in blood gases and other chemicals and indicate whether the respiratory function is matching the need for oxygen.

Cystic Fibrosis Genetic disease that causes thick mucus to be overly secreted and clog the air passages, increasing the risk of respiratory system infections.

Dalton's Law Law that states that the total pressure of a mixture of gases is the sum of the pressures of each gas in the mixture.

Dead Air Air left in the lungs after inspiration that does not contribute to gas exchange in the alveoli.

Diaphragm Muscle that separates the thoracic cavity from the lower abdominal cavity, involved with inhalation.

Diffusion Random movement of molecules from a region of high concentration to a region of low concentration.

Emphysema Disease of the lungs in which the alveoli remain permanently enlarged and the alveolar walls deteriorate, causing the lungs to become less elastic.

Epiglottis Flexible cartilage that extends from the back of the tongue to the thyroid cartilage, and covers the larynx when food or fluid is being swallowed to prevent it from entering the respiratory system.

Esophagus Long, narrow tube of the digestive system that moves partially digested food to the stomach after it is swallowed.

Expiration Phase of breathing when air flows out of the lungs.

Expiratory Center Area in the medulla oblongata that is involved in stimulating the expiratory muscles.

Expiratory Neurons Neurons located in the expiratory center that excite the muscles involved with expiration.

Glossary

Expiratory Reserve Volume Amount of air that can be expired beyond the tidal expiration.

Fick's Law Law that states that the rate that a molecule, such as oxygen, will diffuse from one region to another depends on a number of factors, including the difference in partial pressures between the regions.

Goblet Cells Type of cells that line the nasal cavity and secrete a protective mucus.

Heimlich Maneuver A method of dislodging food or other material from the throat of a person who is choking, named after Henry Jay Heimlich, an American surgeon.

High-Altitude Pulmonary Edema Also known as HAPE, condition in which fluid leaked from the blood in the pulmonary capillaries accumulates in the lungs at high altitude, caused by a rapid ascent to high altitudes. Can lead to shortness of breath and fast heart rate.

Hypoxia State in which a reduced amount of oxygen is supplied to the tissues.

Infant Respiratory Distress Syndrome Also called hyaline membrane disease, disorder occurring in premature infants in which the membrane lining the alveoli lacks surfactant so that they collapse when the person expires.

Inspiration Phase of breathing when air flows into the lungs.

Inspiratory Center Area within the medulla oblongata that regulates the rhythm of breathing.

Inspiratory Neurons Neurons located in the inspiratory center that excite the muscles involved with inspiration.

Inspiratory Reserve Volume Amount of air that can be inspired beyond the tidal volume.

Intercostals Muscles on the ribs that are involved with breathing.

Lactic Acid Fermentation Process during which lactic acid is converted from pyruvic acid during glucose breakdown, occurs during periods of extended muscle activity when oxygen supply is low.

Larynx Also called the voice box, organ made of cartilage located between the trachea and pharynx, provides an opening for air and a route for food and air to pass through to the appropriate channels.

Medulla Oblongata Lowest portion of the brain. Controls internal organs.

MRI (Magnetic Resonance Imaging) Medical imaging technique that uses electromagnetic radiation to obtain images of the body's soft tissues. Useful in diagnosing certain diseases.

Nasal Cavity Internal cavity within the nose through which air enters.

Noble Gases Also known as inert gases, six elements (helium, neon, argon, krypton, xenon, and radon) that have the maximum number of electrons in their outer shell, making it difficult for them to form compounds with other elements easily.

Nose External structure of cartilage and bone that houses the nasal cavity.

Paraventricular Nucleus Prominent part of the hypothalamus. Along with another prominent structure of the hypothalamus, the supraoptic nuclei, is responsible for the synthesis of antidiuretic hormone and oxytocin.

Parietal Pleural Membrane Membrane that lines the thoracic cavity.

Partial Pressure Gradient The difference in pressure of individual gases between two regions of concentration.

Partial Pressures The pressure exerted by each gas in a mixture of gases.

Peripheral Chemoreceptors Sensory receptors that are located in the carotid arteries and the aortic arch.

PET (Positron Emission Tomography) Medical imaging method capable of displaying the metabolic activity of organs in the body. Useful in diagnosing cancers and locating brain tumors.

pH A measure of the hydrogen ion concentration; any pH below 7 is acidic and any pH above 7 is basic.

Pharynx Organ that connects the nasal cavity and mouth to the larynx and esophagus and serves as a pathway for food and air.

Pleura Two-layered membrane that covers the outside surface of the lungs and lines the thoracic cavity.

Pleural Cavity Space that contains a lung.

Pneumotaxic Area Region of the pons in the brain that continuously sends impulses to the inspiratory center of the medulla that control the rate of breathing.

Glossary

Pneumothorax Presence of air in the space between the lungs and the pleural cavity.

Pons Part of the brainstem that connects the medulla to the midbrain.

Pulmonary Edema Condition that occurs as a result of fluid accumulating in the lungs.

Residual Volume Amount of air in the lungs that remains after a person exhales.

Respiratory Bronchioles Small air passages that begin where the terminal bronchioles end, and lead to alveoli sacs, where gas exchange can occur.

Respiratory Membrane Barrier composed of the inside of the alveoli walls, which are type I cells, and the outside of the alveoli walls, which consist of pulmonary capillaries. The membrane has gas on one side and blood on the other side.

Sinuses Cavities in the cranium that are lined with mucus and filled with air.

Spirometer Instrument consisting of a hollow bell inverted over water that measures lung volumes and capacities.

Surface Area Amount of space on the face of an object.

Surfactants Secretions produced by the alveoli that reduce the surface tension of water molecules and prevent the collapse of the alveoli after each expiration.

Tidal Volume Amount of air that can be inspired during normal, restful breathing, amount of air in the lungs that does not participate in gas exchange (dead air) plus the amount of air that reaches the alveoli.

Total Atmospheric Pressure Also known as barometric pressure, the force per unit area exerted against a surface by the weight of the air molecules above that surface. The sum of all the partial pressures.

Total Lung Capacity Sum of all lung volumes (tidal, inspiratory reserve, expiratory reserve, and residual), normally around 6000 ml (6L) in the average male.

Trachea Tube surrounded by cartilage that extends from the larynx to the bronchi.

Tuberculosis (TB) A highly contagious disease caused by a rod-shaped bacterium, *Mycobacterium tuberculosis.*

Type I Alveolar Cells Squamous epithelium cells of the walls of the alveoli.

Type II Alveolar Epithelial Cells Cube-shaped cells on the walls of the alveoli that secrete a fluid containing surfactant that coats the surface of the alveoli.

Visceral Pleural Membrane Membrane that covers the outside surface of the lungs.

Vocal Cords Two muscular folds that vibrate and produce sound as air passes through them.

Bibliography and Further Reading

American Lung Association. "Trends in Air Quality." From the ALA's Best Practices and Program Services, 2002.

American Lung Association. "Trends in Cigarette Smoking." 1999.

American Lung Association Fact Sheets on Asthma, Lung Cancer, Cigarette Smoking, Tuberculosis, and Emphysema. 2002. (*http://www.lungusa.org/diseases*).

Beardsley, T. "Seeing the Breath of Life." *Scientific American,* June 1999.

Campbell, N., and J. Reece. *Biology,* 6th ed. San Francisco: Benjamin Cummings, 2002.

Curtis, R. "Outdoor Action Guide to High Altitude: Acclimatization and Illnesses." Princeton University, 1998. (*http://www.princeton.edu/~oa/safety/altitude.html*).

Earth's Atmosphere. (*http://liftoff.msfc.nasa.gov/academy/space/atmosphere.html*).

Freeman, S. *Biological Science,* 1st ed. Upper Saddle River, NJ: Prentice Hall, 2002.

High Altitude Pulmonary Edema (HAPE). (*http://hypoxia.uchsc.edu:8080/hape.htm*).

Hill, R. "The history of the British Iron Lung 1832–1995." (*http://www.geocities.com/ironlungmuseum/ironlung.htm*).

Hultgren, H. *High Altitude Medicine.* Stanford, CA: Hultgren Publishers, 1997.

Krakauer, J. *Into Thin Air: A Personal Account of the Mount Everest Disaster.* New York: Villard Books, 1997.

Krauskopf, K.B., and A. Beiser. *The Physical Universe,* 10th ed. New York: McGraw Hill, 2003.

"Lung Diseases in Infants and Children." Columbia University College Home Medical Guide. (*http://cpmcnet.columbia.edu*).

Marieb, E. *Human Anatomy and Physiology,* 4th ed. Menlo Park, CA: Benjamin Cummings, 1998.

Martin, L. *Scuba Diving Explained: Questions and Answers on Physiology and Medical Aspects of Scuba Diving.* New York: Mt. Sinai, 1997.

Medlineplus Health Information. Excessive yawning. 2001. (*http://www.nlm.nih.gov/medlineplus*).

Mines, A. *Respiratory Physiology,* 1st ed. New York: Raven Press, 1986.

O'Neil, D. "Human Biological Adaptability: Adapting to High Altitude." 2002. (*http://anthro.palomar.edu/adapt/adapt_3.htm*).

Saladin, K. *Anatomy and Physiology: The Unity of Form and Function*, 1st ed. New York: WCB McGraw-Hill, 1998.

Schmidt-Nielsen, K. *Animal Physiology: Adaptation and Environment*, 4th ed. New York: Cambridge University Press, 1990.

Shier, D., J. Butler, and R. Lewis. *Hole's Human Anatomy and Physiology*, 8th ed. New York: WCB McGraw-Hill, 1999.

Vander, A., J. Sherman, and D. Luciano. *Human Physiology: The Mechanism of Body Function*, 8th ed. New York: McGraw-Hill, 2001.

West, J.B. *Physiological Basis of Medical Practice*, 11th ed. Baltimore: Lippincott, Williams and Wilkins, 1985.

Wong, A. "Why do we yawn when we are tired? And why does it seem to be contagious?" *Scientific American*, 2002. (*http://www.sciam.com/askexpert_directory.cfm*).

WEBSITES

American Lung Association
www.lungusa.org

Canadian Lung Association
www.lung.ca

Centers for Disease Control and Prevention
www.cdc.gov

Information about Positron Emission Tomography
http://subtlebraininjury.com/Pet.html

National Heart, Lung, and Blood Institute
(Department of Health and Human Services/
National Institutes of Health)
www.nhlbi.nih.gov

National Institutes of Health, United States Library of Medicine
www.nlm.nih.gov/medlineplus

World Health Organization
www.who.int

Conversion Chart

Unit (metric)		Metric to English	English to Metric	
LENGTH				
Kilometer	km	1 km 0.62 mile (mi)	1 mile (mi)	1.609 km
Meter	m	1 m 3.28 feet (ft)	1 foot (ft)	0.305 m
Centimeter	cm	1 cm 0.394 inches (in)	1 inch (in)	2.54 cm
Millimeter	mm	1 mm 0.039 inches (in)	1 inch (in)	25.4 mm
Micrometer	µm			
WEIGHT (MASS)				
Kilogram	kg	1 kg 2.2 pounds (lbs)	1 pound (lbs)	0.454 kg
Gram	g	1 g 0.035 ounces (oz)	1 ounce (oz)	28.35 g
Milligram	mg			
Microgram	µg			
VOLUME				
Liter	L	1 L 1.06 quarts	1 gallon (gal)	3.785 L
			1 quart (qt)	0.94 L
			1 pint (pt)	0.47 L
Milliliter	mL or cc	1 mL 0.034 fluid ounce (fl oz)	1 fluid ounce (fl oz)	29.57 mL
Microliter	µL			
TEMPERATURE				
$°C = 5/9 \, (°F - 32)$		$°F = 9/5 \, (°C + 32)$		

Index

Index

Picture Credits

About the Author

Dr. Susan Whittemore is a Professor of Biology at Keene State College in Keene, NH. She received a Master's degree from Utah State University and her Ph.D. in Physiology from Dartmouth Medical School in 1991. She also completed a post-doctoral program in molecular endocrinology at Dartmouth before arriving at Keene State in 1993. Dr. Whittemore teaches a wide range of biology courses for non-majors, including Genetics and Society, Forensic Science, Women and Science, Human Biology, and Human Anatomy and Physiology. In addition, she teaches an introductory Biology course, Research Rotations, Physiology of Plants and Animals, Comparative Animal Physiology, and Ecophysiology. She was a recent recipient of an National Science Foundation grant that provided instrumentation for her work in molecular physiology. She was a contributing author to Scott Freeman's *Biological Sciences* (2002), an introductory biology text published by Prentice Hall.